AUTOBIOGRAPHY OF
JONATHAN ANTHONY BURKETT

My Life, My Story

Autobiography of Jonathan Anthony Burkett

My Life, My Story

Jonathan Anthony Burkett

To order additional copies of this book, contact:
Xlibris Corporation
1-888-795-4274
www.Xlibris.com
Orders@Xlibris.com
52497

People I give thanks to for coming into my life and for every word of encouragement they have given me:

Lynn Burkett (grandmother)
Arnold Burkett (grandfather)
Alexander Archer (brother)
George Archer Jr. (brother)
Marise Christophe (godmother)
Loleth Corpus (friend)
Clara Diez (friend)
Tracie Koonce (friend)
Ingrid Lawrence (friend) and many more

ACKNOWLEDGMENTS

I first give thanks to my Lord and Savior, Jesus Christ, and my Father God, for being right here by my side, day and night, taking me through all my troubled times and hard struggles, through the life I now live. I give thanks for my angel who's been looking over me, who was sent from heaven by my Lord and Savior, Jesus Christ. I give thanks to my Father God for giving me such loving and kind grandparents, brothers, aunties, uncles, and cousins in Jamaica.

I give thanks for my two brothers; I feel no matter what, we will always love one another, be there for one another. They have given me another reason to stay here and live a life here on earth and achieve success in my lifetime.

I give thanks to all of the nurses and doctors who have given love and have supported me in my lifetime, time and time again. I give thanks to Ms. Marise, a worker from memorial hospital, for all the love and support given to me, as if I was her son, even when I was out of the hospital. She inspired me to do right and to go for something in life, and not just sit down, sad and mad at life.

I thank God for all who have supported me with food and love, wanting nothing in return, even though they did not know me, while I was living on the streets. I thank God for my friends who have helped me to a have a place to rest my head at night time and time again, encouraged me to do right in my life, even though I wanted to do whatever I could at times to survive, and letting go was hurting me so drastically in a bad manner.

I give thanks to all those street men who were not doing well at that time, but were still encouraging and teaching me about each consequence for everything we do, and telling me to be the best man that I can be in life and to try to take advantage of each opportunity and chance I get in life, to live a right and astonishing life.

I give thanks to all the people, and all my friends' parents who wanted to be there for me, who still chose to guide me from certain areas, telling me not to follow their older son's actions in life because they did not want me to end up like other friends and family members who never had someone to inspire and encourage them to do better in life, who were also going through similar struggles in their lives.

I give thanks to all the churches for giving my Father's words to me, for making me think more positively, and for making me into a better man. To all the pastors and ministers, for all their strong words of encouragement, saying that if one has faith in one's life, no matter the obstacles and struggles, our Father God will bless him or her in an unbelievably astonishing way.

I give God thanks for bringing that special friend, best friend, and sister into my life. One of the people I felt I loved the most in my life, because she not just approached me with words of being a better person in my life but also taught me to do better, even though I kept doing some wrong in my life. I thank her for her trueness with me and the feelings that I felt from her that made me jiggle and made me feel true love.

I give God thanks for my brothers, the ones who used to sneak me inside the house whenever I needed a shower and food, and whenever they could, a roof and a bed to sleep on at night. I love you all the most.

All I have to say to my mother is I wish someone could have been there for you and I am sorry, for everything. You are my birth mother, and I have love for you and I give thanks for you. However, it had never really been said when it had all finally developed in my mind because of how we have departed from each other's lives.

Again, I give my Lord and Savior, Jesus Christ, and my Father God.

Thanks and praises.

LIFE IN THE VALLEY

This is a life story about me as a young man going through many struggles in life, from losing the one I loved the most in life to having my first mental breakdown in elementary school, and being told, "I wish you would've died" by the one I was told loved me more than my grandfather. Then ending up, at an early age of fourteen, sleeping on the streets, cars, and parks. With a broken heart and mind with the life I was living.

Living with a brain disorder due to stress, I was told, and to anxiety. Asking my Father God, "Will I ever be given love? Will I be truly loved by another in this lifetime of mine?"

INTRODUCTION

I give my Lord and Savior, Jesus Christ, and my Father God an apology every night and day ever since that day I told them that I am now an unbeliever of their works and existence because of what I was going through, with the feeling of having no one there at my side. Still to this day, I do the same because of what I have learned in life.

There has been so many wrong routes that I've taken in my existence because of so much confusion and neglect that my mother has given to me, because of her seeing another every time she catches sight of or gets near me. Why so much hate, so much unwelcome criticism I've been given? I had constantly asked myself, "Am I not your son? Am I that ugly that I frighten you, making you despise me in your life?" I have had so many unbelievable experiences that I feel if I say too much, I will be looked at differently by whosoever reads this book in my lifetime. However, I still feel that I need to let it all out to be able to move toward a better life, because that was what was constantly said to me day by day.

I now say that this is a book with an example of how some people change themselves, because of how they feel they can handle themselves. Therefore, they hold it all in, saying that they can handle it all, never expecting any problems and changes in their minds, with all held inside themselves until another situation occurs and they feel that they cannot take it all anymore, especially when feeling alone and with no one there for them. Therefore, they end up taking their lives. I was always one inch away from doing that myself, and not caring if I made it to heaven or hell.

I have to live a stress-free life now, but how am I going to when I have no one here who will truly love and be there for me day by day? How am I going to make it when I cannot find a job because of my background? Therefore, what am I going to do? I have depression deep inside of me and anger inside of me, and surprisingly, that one love that I felt I would have died for is now out of my life.

That is when I started wanting time by myself. I would sit down quietly, looking out at the highway in front of the complex that I was living in. I wondered how come they are not living a life like mine, no car, no family at my side, no job, no money, no one telling me "I love you," and if I went back to the hospital, no one there to be at my side, waiting for my recovery. Therefore, I started thinking, writing, watching television, and reading my roommate's books, which was something I never liked to do.

"Going through illness, troubled times, death, feeling unloved, being an entrepreneur, writing, hoping to have a great future. Be confident in your approach to success in having a better future. Take risks, try new things for a future, be diligent, and find techniques, and in the end you would develop a compelling emotional element."

I took these words as inspiring words for me, telling me to try things that I have never thought of doing. I have made it through trials, so now let me see if I can make it through challenges in life.

I now want to have the most that I can have in life, with my brothers, my future, my family in life. Therefore, I am now doing the best that I can do in everything that I have the privilege to achieve in life, including my first real book.

CHAPTER 1

Born and raised in Jamaica, John's mother had grown up being loved and supported by all in her mother and father's home, because John's mother was the most loved baby out of all their five children. John's mother was helped and defended in almost all her conflicts and fights that she had experienced during her younger years in life. Even if one member of the household wasn't around, another family member or friend would be around to help defend her. Given money, clothing, and also talked to about many things about one's time in life, John's mother started having in mind her future life goals. Since John's mother always wanted more and wasn't giving up until she was almost getting it all, they began believing in his mother's future in life.

John's mother grew up into a young adult wanting it all, but not knowing how to live earning independently, all her earnings by herself. That I believe was part of the reason why she started messing her life up, by not using her common sense at times, because she was used to jumping before thinking, depending on another. She was also jealous, following others, and wanted more than anyone else.

John's mother was calm and nice to others and didn't expect to ever have to fight for or fight back for anything that she ever wanted or didn't want, because she expected to get babied, even when she was no longer a child.

John's mother had finished school and was working hard making little money for herself somehow and was not only looking as if she was filled with delight, but also telling others that she felt delighted in her life, because she had grown around so much of her family and friends, who loved and cared for her, with all their hearts, souls, and minds.

John's grandmother and grandfather didn't just love his mother, but they also never wanted his aunts or uncles out of their sights either. Why? Because of all the fights, shootings, and killings that was happening in Jamaica. So each one of their children was being loved the same but was treated differently in life because of age and gender.

After hearing about the American life, not only from teachers but also from others, John's mother now began seeing America on television, looking as if it had so much more to offer a person in life. John's mother ended up wanting more happiness and more money in her life, and America just looked like the place for it all.

John's mother wanted better success, more money to earn in her lifetime. So John's mother told her brothers, sisters, and other family members also looking for and wanting success; and they all said yes so they all went to get an American visa, wanting to become a United States citizen. So having help from her friends and family, who were also trying, also wanting to get into the United States of America for outstanding moneymaking careers that they had always wanted, to be able to come back to Jamaica and help out their families and friends.

There was one family member who was already in the United States, who was also trying his best to help, so their family branch could grow in the United States of America. So that one put his time and effort into trying to get John's mother and all the others into the United States of America.

After some time, John's mother and some family members, not all, had successfully gotten their papers for the United States of America, but I guess only for a certain amount of time. So John's mother and all the others who were able to get their papers left as soon as they could, for the United States of America, in Miami, Florida. Where they found someone that they could stay with, who knew someone or was among their family members in Jamaica. So John's mother now finally got in the air to get down to the place where she believed would give and have more for her in her life.

John's mother finally began living, just like any other foreigner from another land, meaning trying to get to know this land that she is now in so that she could survive in it day by day. John's mother then made it through most of her struggles and hard times, because she was trying hard, not giving up, on living a wonderful American life.

John's mother started locating better jobs with better pay and less struggles and made friends to help her and to give all the love she missed from back at home.

John's mother began living with a friend named Nicole who helped her out to get a good job, but they eventually went their separate ways. Nicole had a husband and three children who were living happily with their lives. Nicole was an active lady, shopping and going out a lot on days when she wasn't working. Nicole's husband Mario was an all-work-and-no-play kind of guy but at times still had some fun calm days doing things with his wife, children, or friends.

John's mother started becoming jealous, wanting that same kind of man holding her and present in her life. So she started going out and going on dates but still never found that one for some time.

Mario and Nicole's home ended up needing some maintenance done after some time, so it became a time of anger because John's mother of course had to help out. It was John's mother home also, so it was understandable at that time, but money for John's mother was coming to her only as she worked. She had to start shopping less because she had to help Mario and Nicole out in certain areas of their home. John's mother was unhappy at first, until one of the men that were working on their home maintenance said that he liked her. He asked her out on a date, just the two of them together.

It was a wonderful night of happiness, and enchanting stories were all John's mother was bringing back home on their dinner table the next day, wanting to get the married couple jealous, it seemed like. Well, at least she tried; but Mario and Nicole still had it better because Mario didn't just want sex from Nicole whenever they were alone together.

John's mother continued talking to him and began loving him after sometime because he was such a fast moneymaking man. One night, John's mother came back home after a special night with that man, sad and looking abused, saying, "Tonight will be the last night I'll ever spend with that man."

She did not tell anyone how, why, when, where, and who gave her certain marks in her body because of all the embarrassment and pain she felt deep inside, hiding and holding it all in, away from anyone. John's mother tried to forget about that man and what he did to her that night because it was all bringing her down.

John's mother had then gotten pregnant but never thought she was at first. She never went to the doctor and had herself tested for pregnancy and for AIDS and HIV.

John's mother then finally had it in her to tell one of her friends, named Lisa, about it. Lisa wanted to know what happened to her awesome relationship with that man. John's mother truly trusted Lisa, so she told her what happened. Lisa then told her to immediately go and get tested for pregnancy because she could've easily gotten pregnant since he didn't use a condom.

It then became too late for the baby to be aborted when the doctor told John's mother that she was pregnant. Plus she didn't have the money and support for certain things like that.

She was not happy with who the father of her first child was and who she was about to give birth to. She was happy and excited though that she now had a good reason to stay in the United States of America, once she reports it to the United States government.

The baby was born in Miami, Florida, on February 1, 1987, and named Jonathan Anthony Burkett, by whom? He doesn't know. He was not wanted or cared for by his mother because of the memories of that man. John's mother asked her mother if John could stay with them in Jamaica because she was still struggling in America. However, John's mother never told John's grandparents how she had gotten pregnant and then had him.

John was sent to Jamaica to live with his grandparents, the parents of his aunts, uncles, and his mother, the ones John truly felt are his mother and his father because of the love and care they gave him every day, all the days and years he was right there with them in Jamaica and John knows even now.

John had grown up with his grandmother and her mother, his great-grandmother, and his grandfather who was also John's brother, best friend, father, and cousin all in one. John's grandfather was the one he knew who was forever going to love him and appreciate his days with him.

Living with his grandparents, John was very happy, and he felt he was treated like one of the best persons in their lives.

John could always think back to nothing else but happy thoughts and times when he was growing up with his grandparents. Also of course his aunts, uncles, and cousins because they were at John's side each and every day of the week, playing and feeding him, making him feel loved and appreciated.

John loved being in Jamaica because of the food, long nights of music and dancing, freedom, and family.

Johnny was his name in the streets up until he started to do bad things; then Bad Boy Johnny was the name one would hear about in the streets. John was always walking around the streets and climbing hills because he loved to stay active even though he was doing wrong at times.

John had all kinds of family members, young and old, women and men, around him all the time because he was always in the street with or without his grandfather or cousins at his side. So good, bad, crazy, and wild grew into Johns' life and mind, and it all ended up growing in him the more he was with his cousins, the ones who were watching over him most of the time.

John's cousins used to do the same bad things around him as if he was never there. Whenever his cousins were with their girlfriends, John kept getting told to close his eyes and not open them until one cousin said that they were finished. John used to watch them night and day as his cousins did things with their friends and girlfriends.

Rough Jamaican male attitudes had grown in John's personality the more his cousins would scream at him and then loving him by wanting him near, not far. Therefore, from being quiet, to being loud, crazy, and very energetic, John was turning into a different person day by day. It all mattered, of course, how the day before had gone and the kind of dreams John would have in the middle of the night. His dreams had him sometimes scared and always wetting his bed.

John used to have scary ghost dreams because of television, which is why he never got interested in watching television so much except for dance-hall tapes because that was when the woman would be teaching him how to dance like them.

John's superman, best friend, and grandfather used to sleep with him at nighttime, to make sure no one scared him or captured him and then took him away. A lot of that happened in Jamaica but mostly to the beautiful girls.

John loved his grandfather so much. They were like brothers, so John never called him grandfather; he called his grandfather Doctor because that was his grandfather's nickname in the streets. John's grandfather always loved to care and help out others as much as he could which was why he was called "Doctor."

John's grandfather used to sleep with him every night even though he used to wet the bed at nighttime; and if he could not sleep, John's grandfather stomach was his comfort and something he could hold at night. His stomach was big but very comfortable.

As John slept at night, he moved up and down so comfortably as if someone had him in his or her arms rocking him.

John used to always look at it and wonder if that is how big his stomach was going to be when he got old like his grandfather. John's grandmother loved her husband's stomach too, rubbing on it, making jokes about it, saying, "Johnny, you're about to have another uncle."

John's grandmother had her own room with designs, curtains, and a fan above her bed. She used to go after him whenever he went to her bed especially at nighttime because she didn't want him sleeping on her bed at all, so he was given a line that he couldn't cross or else he would have to run.

Growing up in Jamaica, John never had to fear a beating because all he had to do was scream out for his grandfather or run to his grandfather, and his grandfather would come and save him from all his days and nights of trouble. That was what really made his grandfather his superman.

John had learned a lot about doing good and not bad from his grandmother and grandfather but still did not really care until his grandmother started locking him inside of the house. Nevertheless, John still did whatever, whenever, because all he had to do was call his grandfather and his grandfather would help him and then talk to John about the things he was doing wrong.

John used to go out with his grandfather a lot because he was a taxi driver and John loved driving. Mario go-carts were not enough for John; he wanted to feel more. So whenever he went out with his grandfather, he began sitting in the driver's seat with his grandfather. Therefore, there were two drivers, so that meant four hands on just one steering wheel.

John used to be the driver on his lap, listening to the music, moving up and down. While his grandfather was pressing down on the gas and brake pedal, John would be moving around and sometimes standing on his grandfather's lap dancing to the music.

John loved being with his grandfather because there was only one thing he would ever say no to him about doing, and that was smoking cigarettes. He even used to let him take little sips of beer and rum, which of course would then put him straight to sleep. John could not even remember how they got back into their bed those nights after just one sip of his grandfather's drink.

Holding John close one day on his lap, John's grandfather told him,

> I love you and will be with you always, Johnny. One says I hate you; remember, Johnny, I love you. You ever need me, please call me, I am here for you. Do not run from any man or problems or else many more may come to you so face them all, one at a time, for all may come at once one day and then it may become much harder to defeat them all. Speak and not hold back inside, one wants to fight, do not run because my fists are your fists. Do you see how big they are? Use them, but do not bully with them. Wrong or right, I will still be there for you; just be a truthful young man, with me, your grandmother, aunts, uncles, and many others. It will bring you far in life and sometimes down in your life, but still being truthful with me, consequences may not take part. I am here for you, and I love you like no other will ever do; even when I am gone, I will love you still, Johnny, just remember me and what I have said. I will never forget you, Johnny, and I will always love you, and again, Johnny, I love you, remember, so smile. I, Arnold E. Burkett, love you, and I am in you for the rest of my life and your life even after, and you, Jonathan Burkett, are free to come to me any day you choose to. One more thing, Johnny, even if you have to put me aside, just remember to "Put your Father God first" in all of your lifetime and on.

Hurricane season was one of the greatest times in their streets because they were up so high on a hill, their crossroads were packed up with everyone naked, both boys and girls, young and old, because they would all be able to have long hours of showers. Walking around with soap in their hands and running around in all the streets and yards, naked, looking for girls and boys, making loud noises, playing hide-and-seek—that's all they used to do and not even soap up themselves.

Those times were like some of the best times in John's life and he feels may always be one of his happiest times. Then after the rain, most of them would be stuck in their homes with a cold that they all ended up catching because of such long showers at certain times of the days.

When John began his first year in school, he did not want at all to be there because he felt no freedom at all. Locked in a room, sitting down, and not being able to get up without his teacher's permission made him just start wanting to do something to get kicked out. So John used to throw things at his teachers, but then instead of his teacher telling him to leave, because she knew he wanted to and because he was the only student not drawing and coloring pictures, the teacher just had John behind her in the corner until he was ready to start participating in class activities.

The one thing John loved to do though was to go outside and play. The school used to all play football (soccer) and cricket together. John would not even smile even while he was having fun. Fights occasionally occurred because he was always told to never allow another man to put their hands on him. Then it would get him to detention, but one day at his detention, the teacher asked him what he was interested in and he said playing football. She continued talking to him about different things in life, and even a private sex class, in class and at her home. From that day and on, John always had it his way in class because she never wanted him to tell his grandmother about what happened.

Whenever John saw fights on the streets, it influenced him to stand up for himself and fight back if another messed with him. But then again he used to wonder why? Most of the men's enemies would lie down in that one spot and never get back up. He asked himself if they were killed like the animals we kill to eat, because whenever he asked his uncles, they would just be like, "That person is just sleeping on the floor, Johnny, because they have nowhere else to sleep."

CHAPTER 2

John's sixth birthday was just around the corner since they all had just reached a new year and that was the year 1993, so his grandfather planned a big birthday party for him on February 1 in the crossroad, at nighttime. Many people ended up finding out from their children and their friends' children about bad boy Johnny's first big birthday party in the crossroad.

Before the party, John's grandfather took him out to go and get some new clothing so that he could have been showing all the girls what he got and then making them want him. John had gotten new shoes, also a nice pretty haircut, even though he was far from one because John was really just looked at as a young street bad boy, not a fashionable young boy.

When John and his grandfather had finally gotten back, the crossroad was setup with all the speakers and the DJ's big place to make the girls go wild.

As soon as 8:00 p.m. came, everybody started coming and dropped off because there were no cars allowed in the crossroad for that night. Everybody first went over to John, wishing him a happy birthday and wanting to cut the cake before the music started playing because once it started, they said they won't stop.

John's presents ended up being women dancing because that was what John loved seeing, but this day for him was going to be more than sight. It became an overcrowded party because many people that John was not even expecting to come just came telling him that he was no longer a baby so it was time to begin partying and growing into a young man.

There were adult women, men, and young kids just dancing, trying to compete with John because it was his birthday party. Therefore, John was dancing with grown Jamaican women that he could not even keep up with because of their fast moves on him and he was smaller and skinnier than they all were.

John's grandfather, uncles, and their friends were just drinking and playing dominoes in one corner, having fun with one another. All John's cousins and friends were in the middle of the crossroad dancing with all the women who were there dancing alone because John could not handle them all.

That night was when John finally started releasing his feelings, hands, and kisses on females because he finally overcame that fear in him, so now he felt like he could tell a girl he did not know that he liked her and wanted her to be his girlfriend.

Two in the morning came, and everybody kept telling John that his grandmother was looking for him now. Therefore, he started running and hiding from her because he already knew that she wanted him inside. His grandmother could not catch him, so she called his aunties to come and help her because everybody else would have been working with John to get away.

When she had finally caught John, his grandmother was mad at him because all she really wanted to do was just to check to see if he was doing OK.

Therefore, she told John that he had to go to bed now since he was running away from her and making her worry about him. He had gotten angry because everybody was still outside dancing and partying for his birthday, without him anywhere near.

John just began lying down on his bed with clothes and shoes still on, listening to the music play and everyone making noise because he was mad and couldn't even sneak out because she was sleeping on the couch in front of his bed.

John could not sleep because of so much of them girls he had in his mind, so he was awake until eight in the morning. He then got up and went back outside without even asking his grandmother, who was still sleeping on the couch. John was somewhat upset because he was seeing his DJ and his DJ friends pick up all their speakers to leave.

Before they had left, they had seen John watching them, so they walked over to him and wished him a happy birthday again before they left and told him that next time he will be able to stay all night with all the women dancing and doing the butterfly. However, John was saying that he did not even get a girlfriend, so the DJ told him that all those girls last night was his girlfriend because the DJ had never gotten as much kisses as John was getting in one night. The whole DJ crew had then left, with John sitting down thinking about what went on after he left.

John had just turned six years old and had, had such a surprisingly big birthday party. However, he did not know that there were more surprises coming for him, surprises that John never even dreamed about or even thought of because of course he was still very young. However, John never really wanted another person in his life except his first girlfriend.

Unexpectedly, John's birth father came for him out of nowhere one day in Jamaica to bring him back home to Miami, Florida. His aunts had known that his father was coming but not his grandparents, because they were also so surprised, and it was their first time meeting John's father ever since John had been born.

John's grandparents had then called John to introduce him to his father, but John did not even want to get to know him at all. John was disrespectful to him because he did not want him anywhere near him or talking to him.

The next couple of days, John's grandmother told him that he was leaving, so he had to go and say good-bye to all of his cousins, aunts, uncles, and friends.

At last, of course, he also had to say good-bye to his grandparents. John's great-grandmother, who was always quiet and wondering about him, gave him a big hug and told him that she loved him and to never forget about her because she never knew when her last day on earth was going to be. His grandmother was telling him to go up to Miami respecting his parents and loving them the same way that he loved them.

Nevertheless, John's grandfather did not want him to leave even though he needed freedom in his life now because he was getting older. Therefore, John hugged his grandfather and told him that when he comes back he better be here, so he said OK as long he respected his mother and father, whom he was going to go and live with.

John had forgotten all about saying good-bye to his teacher, so he ended up going to her thirty minutes before he left that day. His teacher told him to go and be thankful because he was going where she wished she were because she was afraid of all the aggressive men, diseases, and infections in Jamaica. Then she told John that she was just trying to let him get her pregnant so that she could have gotten a greater chance to go to America because she found out John was born in America. Still all John did was just say good-bye, wondering why he has to get her pregnant so that she could get to America.

John ended up wetting his pants and throwing up on his first flight home because of a ringing in his ears and that funny feeling in him that he felt while he was eating but just decided to ignore it. "We have landed safely," John had then finally heard, with everybody applauding and smiling except for him.

Coming off the plane and then into an airport, John had to change his clothes because he had already had the airplane smelling bad and himself worse.

John was not really expecting everything that he was seeing as they walked to get their luggage, shoes on every man's feet, electronics, and computers everywhere. Walls were painted well and looked clean, with all kinds of pictures, designs, and colors. Everyone and everything were looking very clean, polished, and organized for the first time. They remind me of my grandmother, John was saying in his mind.

When John and his father went outside, John did not see any trees or any bushes around. Is there any food here? John asked himself because he wasn't seeing anything natural being grown, nothing but cars and people screaming for cars while cars were blowing their horns at the people.

John was not even paying attention to anyone, not even the ones that came and picked him and his father up. John just wanted to go back to his great-grandmother, grandmother, and grandfather because he was not interested in any other than them.

John had only been in two different cars so far in his lifetime. So now, this car was the third one and it was very different, he was thinking in his mind, because everything in that car that he was in looked new. John had never sat in the back seat of a car before, only in the back of a pickup truck. Therefore, it felt different for him looking at another driver and especially with no loud music and no one screaming out in the back seat where they wanted him and his grandfather to stop at.

"Hello, how are you doing?" a woman named Nicole asked John. He thought that she was his mother at first, but she was not. She was just the woman that John's mother asked to help her to start a great American life.

Nicole had a husband whose name was Mario and they had three children, two boys and one girl. Nicole's two sons, Clinton, sixteen years old, and Gary, twenty years old, have straight street-life minds, having fights every night and day except for Sundays of course because Sunday is one of the Lord's day to give him thanks and praises, so they would all go to church. Her daughter Latoya, who was seventeen years old, grew up loving and into school but at the same time partied from night until dawn with her friends.

John had gotten real close with Nicole and her family before his own mother because he did not see his mother until about five weeks later. John used to take Nicole as his mother, so her home was his home because he was treated just like Nicole was his mother—because she would beat him and punish him, just like how he would see and hear Clinton and Gary get a beating except sometimes she would be telling them to get out of her children's rooms while she was going in with a belt. Then John would be hearing them get a beating, but their beatings did not make any sense because all it did was just make Clinton and Gary madder and wanting to fight another.

One day, John told Nicole that he did not have enough clothes to last for two weeks because Nicole only allowed them to wash every two weeks because they did not want their water bill going up any higher. Therefore, Nicole called John's father about it all, and he then dropped off some clothing for his son to wear.

John continued to be an active young boy, as if he was still in Jamaica, like sneaking out the house, whenever he was told not to go outside, and then also he would sneak his young friends in Nicole's house whenever he wasn't supposed to because no one was around to watch him and his friends.

All of John's friends were mostly Clinton's and Gary's friends' little brothers or cousins who lived with them. All they used to do was play football and watch as their brothers or their brothers' friends fight other people in the streets; and then when they got back to where John was staying, they all would have an aggressive backyard brawl, with John always getting beat up because he was always the youngest.

One night, Clinton was supposed to be watching John but instead went on a date with one of his girls. John caught one of his friends watching Latoya as she was changing in the room with her friends because they were about to go to a party.

However, instead of John telling him to get back in Clinton's room, he watched right alongside with them until they got spotted. They ran back into Clinton's room, but Latoya came to them and told them that they did not have to run; but she wanted to know how long they were watching them. John told her that they had just gotten there; Latoya then told them, "Do not look at me, but you can look at them," which were her friends because they did not care.

However, it was not every time John got away with all the bad things he would do, so whenever John would be caught doing wrong. Nicole would go after John with her belt, but Clinton and Gary would take him and run whenever they saw Nicole going after John.

Then at nighttime, when they knew that Nicole, their mother, would be looking for John, they made him sleep either in the shower or in one of their room closets because no one could've locked a door in that house except for Latoya because she always had a friend sleeping over at night. However, Clinton and Gary have never had a friend sleep over with them at night.

Why did none of Clinton's or Gary's friends not have the privilege to be in Nicole's home? Because of how much trouble they get into, because of the type of people they were. However, Clinton and Gary would have their friends over the house at nighttime. When their mother and father were not around, it was always like a party going on, without Nicole's permission, but they would not find out until some of their favorite liquor bottles were finished.

Nicole used to try to get John to snitch on Gary and Clinton whenever she suspected they did something wrong. However, he never did because then they would beat him up and then punish him by putting him in one of the cars' trunk for some time.

Nicole's home reminded John so much of his grandparent's house in Jamaica, with so much liquor bottles in their house. At first no, he kept getting told, but after a time Latoya began letting John drink it whenever she got tired of him bothering her while she was with her friends or boyfriend and if also she had a lot of homework to do.

Clinton and Gary never actually studied books like Latoya; all they would do was lock John in another room. Whenever their girls came to the house after school or whenever else, and if I came out I would have gotten, bruised up.

John used to talk and walk in the streets also at times with Gary, Clinton, and their friends, night and day, like he used to in Jamaica with his friends and family. However, John had a curfew in Miami; he had to be in the house by at least ten o'clock because of what used to go on at night in their streets. However, he never complained, he just looked out of the windows at nighttime hoping not to miss a fight.

He was never scared in Miami, and he did not want to ever leave Nicole's family home because he was feeling unwanted by his father, that just used to stop by once in a while with some person just looking at him.

One day, that same person that just used to stare at John constantly whenever that person went over Nicole's house went up to John and said, "Let's go, Jonathan."

So John was like, "Where?" "Home," that person then said. "But I am home," John then said. "No, you are not home, Nicole's house is not your home," that person kept on telling John. Nevertheless, John would not listen.

Therefore, that same person had to go and get Nicole to deal with John.

Then when Nicole came, Nicole told John to get up and start getting ready because that person was his mother. "The one that gave birth to you," Nicole told him, "so respect and listen to her before I beat you."

John hurried up and had then gotten ready to go, with his real mother this time. His mother had then taken him to a house that she and her husband had just gotten. John did not ever expect to ever live with another because he was already feeling like he was living with his mother and father and with his two brothers and sister.

The house that they had taken him to was nothing similar to the house that he was living in before especially because it only had two rooms, with no master bedroom. John stayed in his room most of the time unless he saw his father come home because he was already a little familiar with him.

His father was always working and never around, just coming home resting, and paying bills. However, his mother seemed to have had wants, and no love for him, or even interest in parenting him, and not even wanting to feed him in their home. John would always have to wait until his father came home for food to be willingly given to him from his mother.

John was bad at talking; everybody understood that because he still had that attitude and Jamaican accent in him, like whenever he had conversations with adults or even kids his age. John would just speak and say bad things, and John would always ask why. He speaks the way he does.

John was lazy whenever it came down to house chores but not lazy to walk the streets all night and day. But everybody understood the reason why.

He ignored most of the things his mother would tell him not to do in her house because he used to like to explore and touch things that he was not supposed to be touching. Whenever his mother and father bought new things for their new home, he would explore them and then end up breaking them.

However, John was not bad enough for his mother not to love him though, because John always wanted someone to tell him what and who his mother was seeing whenever she looked at him, because she would always go from a serious face, whenever he would break things, to a sad face, with her head down.

One night for the first time since they all moved in together, John's mother just started crying when he was looking at her around their kitchen table, because they were eating dinner that she brought home from Nicole's home. So from then on, John could not eat beside her or across from her, his father told him. John had to eat across his father, who usually sat on the end of their six-chair table.

Nicole started telling John's mother to stop fearing him, when she found out about that night from John's father. She ended up crying and scared because of memories. Therefore, Nicole told John's mother that she needed to start being a real woman and a real mother toward John.

First, she had to spend less time with her friends and raise her firstborn because she was a grown woman now with responsibilities for her child and husband. Second, she needed to start cooking every night now for her husband, because her husband was out there working hard for all three of them in that home. Therefore, she needed to stop going to Nicole's house and taking their dinner home to her man because Nicole also has a hard-working husband to also feed at night.

So John's mother tried then after her talk with Nicole to start to control John and his behavior problems, but his mother could not handle it because she was afraid of John hitting her. John used to curse back at her without even knowing it because that was how he was used to talking and hearing others talked, similar to how he talked.

Therefore, John's mother went back to Nicole again for more advice on raising John.

John's mother went back telling Nicole that she did not know what to do about it all anymore because John would curse back at her, if she ever screamed at him, or told him to get something done in the house. John still never looked at her as a mother, and had never called her "Mother" since he had met her. Because he had never looked at his mother the same as how he has grown up looking at his grandmother.

Nicole, though, was more looked at as a mother to him because she would be there teaching him right from wrong in her eyes and then punishing him.

That was why Nicole told John's mother to drop him off for a couple of days again. Nicole then started telling John right from wrong again, and how to be a good and a respectful child because he was scaring his mother too easily with just one look. Because if she would have gotten a belt to beat John, if John jumped, she jumped, and if John grabbed the belt from her, she would just run in her room and then lock her room door.

John's mother was always so frightened of John. Why? Obviously, she always thought of John as that person from her past.

As a young aggressive child, of course John was going to take advantage of all his chances of not getting a beating by no other except Nicole.

John's mother was so scared of what he was going to do to her one day after John had gotten back from Nicole's house, because she had hit him like how Nicole had told her to do, and John had gotten very mad. So John's mother left him home alone because his father did not reach home yet, and she slept at Nicole's home with Latoya, Nicole's daughter.

The next day John's father had dropped him over at Nicole's house, but they did not know that he had been dropped off because they were locked in the room talking with one another.

In the kitchen, John overheard a conversation going on, with his name spoken aloud constantly. Therefore, John went to the door and then lay down on the floor and listened to the conversation with both his mother and Nicole screaming.

John's mother was crying in the room, asking Nicole, that friend that had introduced his father to his mother, for advice. She said, "I would do whatever you tell me to do because you have been the best friend I ever had in my life."

Nicole was a great friend of course to John's mother, but every friend has a good or bad secret waiting to be revealed, and because of the things John was hearing he wanted badly to reveal the ones he knew about.

Like when John caught Nicole and his father locked in not only Nicole's room but also Nicole's husband's room, and aside from them, only John was around the house, and they thought John had gone back outside. However, John had never gone because he wanted to play Clinton's video game since he was not around to tell him that he could not touch it.

But now when John needed to use the bathroom, he had already known that they were in the room talking, but it sounded like a little more now when he passed by. So John leaned up against the door to hear what it was and it sounded like the noises that his cousins used to make the girls make, whenever they were making out with one another. Nevertheless, John always thought that it was something else because they were both married, and did not they know one another's spouse?

However, it still all had John thinking that Nicole was in there with her husband, but then when he came out the restroom, he saw his father coming out of there and Nicole going in the shower, screaming at him to turn his head.

Then another day, Nicole was up and against John's father, when he had come around the corner, to ask if he was ready because he wanted to go and play outside.

John was there looking at them, but then he had been screamed at to get away from them and not to tell anyone or else she would beat him.

So that means she also had feelings for my father and loved my father because they were always looking like best friends even though she had a husband that she loved, with three children. However, my father only had one child and was married.

CHAPTER 3

Nicole told John's mother to stop being so afraid of him and to release all that anger and hate out on John. All that hate and anger that John's mother had for that man that brought John into her life, Nicole was telling her to release it, and because she was not able to fight back that night, start fighting back right now. Nicole kept telling John's mother, "Remember he did not want to listen that night, well, now make him listen and get him to know that you are not a woman to mess with."

Nicole kept telling John's mother to take it all out on him, but while John was listening, he was wondering why and what person. John did not understand because his mother and his father never argued, because they hardly talked, so they had a calm little-baby relationship going on.

John's mother's attitude, mind, and talk just were getting more outrageous in there, and John began getting scared just from outside the door. It all mainly sounded like John's mother was tremendously hyped up for a death match of some sort.

Then John ran when he heard them walking toward the door. His mother then just came out Nicole's room and screamed out, "Jonathan, get over here now! Get all your things together because we are going home."

"I am tired of your attitude and bad habits," John's mother told John. "I am going to have you start respecting me and listening to whatever I tell you to do, you heard me? Whenever you do something bad, I am going to beat you until you learn not to do it no more. You pee the bed I bought you, you sleep on the floor until you learn."

"So get in the car, and I am going to start hitting you from now, and when we get home, I am going to beat you for all the lies you have told to me and Nicole," John's mother told to John.

When John and his mother had gotten into the car, John was about to snitch on Nicole and his father because he heard Nicole talking behind his back. Therefore, he was going to get her back for all that she was telling his mother.

So now when John and his mother left Nicole's driveway, John said, "I got something to tell you" but his mother told him to shut up and for him not to say another word to her. So now in his mind, he was saying that he should have told her. However, that was just how John's family taught and grown him up in Jamaica because when one talks, one goes and if one keeps his or her mouth shut, that one lives and breathes another day.

"Take off all your clothes," John's mother said to him when they had finally reached home, while she went to go and get a belt from out of my room. Waiting in his room for her, John began laughing because it was looking and seeming as if she was acting.

When John's mother had gotten inside of his room, John's mother then told John, "Get in the corner. Face the wall and close your eyes. She then put John's socks that he just taken off in his mouth and told him that if he came out, she was going to kill him.

Out of nowhere with John's eyes closed, *Whop!* "Jonathan, you're going to learn from your mistakes." *Whop!* "You are no longer going to be disrespecting me in my home." *Whop!* "You are a child and I am an adult so you have to listen to me." *Whop!* Then John had just dropped on the floor crying and telling his mother that he was going to kill her. "What?" his mother said. *Whop, whop, whop, whop, whop, whop, whop!*

Then John's mother went into the kitchen, had gotten a knife and then gave it to him, telling him that if he wants to kill her, this was his chance. However, John said no! Because he knew that his mother was going to go back and tell his grandparents, the ones that he told that he would never kill anyone like how someone had done before, someone that he loved.

Then his mother put it in his face, telling him that if he does not listen, he will find out what is going to happen to him.

This all happened one week before John started first grade. John started first going to Sunshine Elementary School from 1993 to 1994 for his first-grade class.

However, before classes started, John's mother kept telling him that when school starts not to tell anyone that she hits him or else she would beat him when he gets home.

When John began elementary school, he kept on getting into more and more trouble because he never wanted to do any of his schoolwork.

She then started hitting him again, but occasionally stopped, that's why one day he tried to run through the front door but he couldn't because she held on to his shirt and dragged him back in the house. Then John made his way in the bathroom and locked himself in there for about two hours. His mother then ended up breaking down the bathroom door to get him and then started beating him.

Then she made up a lie, telling her husband it was because she thought something happened to John in the bathroom so she had to break it down, because she was worried about him, and she told John that if he told his father what really happened, he was going to get his life beaten out of him.

Every day, even if John did not come home with a bad report, she would beat him, telling him that she hates him.

Every Friday was when all first graders would be taken outside for recess, but John was too bad that week, so his teacher put him in a corner in another classroom with older kids.

He was bored and feeling lonely there, because that class of like twenty kids was so quiet and doing their class work. John started looking around the classroom because that classroom had interesting pictures around it, like big stomachs with little babies inside of them, so it all made him wonder. If it was all true about his grandfather, because he had a big stomach that he used to sleep on. However, he never said that he had a baby growing in there and if he did, he wondered if it came out yet, so then John wanted to call him and then ask his grandfather if it was all true.

John went home still with that question in his mind, but he then ended up asking his mother and if that was where he came out of and how. John's mother then just looked at him and started hitting him the hardest that she could have with her hanger that she had in her hand because she was doing laundry. John just ended up lying down on the kitchen floor not moving but still in pain, with tears still coming down his eyes. She went back in her saying your wanting babies' right instead of holding onto the metal part of the belt. John's mother held on to the other side and just went over him while he was still on the floor. John's mother ended up hitting his knee, back, and head with a meaning behind of it all. John then spent the whole weekend in bed, with all his mother's friends thinking that he had gotten into a fight in school.

After the weekend passed, John ended up still going to school in pain, limping because of his knee and covering up his head, with its big bump that hurts.

John started having many chores in and out the house every day, with ten hits with his mother's belt daily. Until he starts doing everything and behaving right in his mother's house and speaking when allowed to.

Including being the house cleaner and then for his father, day and night as his servant, because his mother never wanted to act wifely toward her husband, so John had to do it.

John had to start taking off shoes for his father whenever he came home from work and sat down around his computer. John had to offer anything around that he could have given to him like food, grapes, or juice. Then after a while, John's father would eventually fall asleep. Then John would be able to go on his daily break.

All John would end up doing was just sit down on the couch and watch television and eat the food that his father left behind because that was the only time that he could've eaten any of his mother's household food.

John was not feeling good one day, so he just came home from school, went in his room, and fell asleep. He forgot all about cleaning and serving his father that day; his father understood why. However, when John's mother came home and saw John sleeping and her husband making his own food to eat, she had gotten mad.

John's father had told her why but she did not care, so she waited until her husband fell asleep.

John's mother then started beating John, telling him that she does not care if he was sick and dying, "No matter what, I want you to be feeding your father and working until you drop down and die in my house."

John's mother then dragged him outside naked and crying, not realizing and remembering that he was already used to being outside naked, and that he loved to walk the streets naked. However, the only thing was that he loved it more while it rains.

Therefore, when she came back outside, she saw him in the backyard, on the grass throwing the ball in the air, playing catch, not caring that neighbors were looking at him, and acting as if he had clothes on his back.

Then December came, and the temperature had dropped. It was like punishment already for John to go outside even with his clothes on, so every weekend he was happy that he did not have to go back outside, so early in the morning times.

"Jonathan, I hope you did not think I forgot about what I said after that day you had a wonderful time outside naked. So let us see if you can handle it, outside naked tonight," John's mother said to him one Friday night.

That night was the coldest, but it ended up being John's bed that night. He was freezing cold, shivering, thinking he was about to freeze to death. However, when John saw the sun rising after hours of not being able to sleep because of such weather he was not used to and did not even know South Florida had.

It was now Saturday, and John knew his father was going to leave their house before seven a.m., so he went around the front yard to knock on the front door, to tell him to let him in now.

Surprisingly, he saw no car in the driveway and he already knew that his mother was not coming back home again until like nighttime before his father got home. Because his father wouldn't have allowed his mother to have done that to him, because every other time that his father found out where John's mother had him, his father had always opened the door and told him to get into the house.

That was why John began always wanting his father around him, so that his father could have helped him out of his situations with his mother.

John started asking his father if he could have started going to work with him, like whenever he had no school because he did not want to be at home alone with his mother anymore.

John's father never screamed at him, no matter how much trouble he had gotten in at school. John's teachers began loving him, especially when he had reached second grade because he would always have them and the class laughing, but sometimes he went too far with the words he would say.

John continued coming home with bad grades on his interim reports and being punished for a couple of days by his mother. However, all John used to have to do was just suck up to his father to get off punishment. John's father used to love purple grapes so John used to prepare them for his father in a bowl every day and night, at whatever time his father got home and wanted them.

John's father was a nice, peaceful man who used to love to watch the Florida Marlins play, "day and night." So he always would watch their games day and night, so that was one of the only times in a day John could have watched television peacefully with his mother home.

John was not allowed to watch television in the house when it would just be him and his mother because all she would be wanting John to do was work, cleaning up every part of the house. Then if there were nothing else around for John to do, she would give him a book to read and then tell him to write a long essay about what he had just read.

John just started to read the same book all the time, and then just gives his mother the same sheet of paper repeatedly if she did not throw away that sheet of paper. John would have always made sure that he had a copy of that same book report because she never used to actually find time to sit down and read what he wrote about his little Daffy Duck books.

John was not a 100 percent good boy, not even a 50 percent good boy. He still used to curse because he did not truly think of his mother and father still as real parents. Just grown adults growing him up in America, they were more like cousins to him especially because of their marriage. Their relationship was more of a sister-and-brother relationship because he had not seen them once get close with one another except in their wedding pictures that were hanged up on the wall. That is part of the reason why John felt the way he felt and did some of the things he did.

John would sneak and do wrongs things in that time just to survive, certain things like sneaking food in his room or outside and going around the house and eating it. He was not allowed to really touch their food whenever they were not around, and so John did what he had to do to survive.

John used to collect every quarter, dime, or nickel that he saw and put it right inside of his book bag for the next day of school so that he could buy candy at school for himself, and Wednesdays were ice cream day, so he would buy ice cream for himself.

They called that stealing, but he still had that Jamaican personality to do whatever he had to do to get what he needed, to survive. John used to get beatings because he used to drink all the strawberry milkshake syrup, because he never used to like the plain milk his mother demanded him to drink on the weekends.

Then all of a sudden John's mother started getting quiet in the house, locking herself in the room, and telling John she doesn't want to be bothered. John's father started sleeping on the bottom bunk bed that he had, and he did not know why.

Then John's father ended up moving into John's room with all his clothing and shoes, in his room.

So that's why John started staying home more and not asking to go over Nicole's house anymore especially when John's mother would have her friends over their house, talking to her about some incident that had just recently occurred.

John had found out what happened when he had reached home first one day from school. When John's mother came home not expecting John to be in the house because she had taken his key away from him, because she did not want him letting anyone in the house that she did not want in there.

However, John had found an extra house key already one day when he was cleaning up his father's room, which was mainly his. John heard his mother talking to one of her friends about why she was so sad and what she had seen to make her feel that way.

John's mother was telling her friend that she found out that her husband was cheating on her with her best friend that she also believed was her sister.

John's mother began crying in front of her friend. Asking her friend why her life had to continuously end up with problems and it all breaking her heart repeatedly.

John then began feeling guilty because he knew his father was cheating on his mother. However, he never had told her because of the way she was treating him every time she was around him, and looking at him, telling John that she hated him.

John had then walked out the door to tell her that it was true because he saw them too, but every time he wanted to say something, especially when he was mad at Nicole, his mother always told him to shut up. In addition, he had gotten threaten that if he had said anything he would not like the consequences for it.

However, as soon as his mother saw John coming out of the room, she just got up and asked him how he got into her house without her knowing.

Therefore, John told his mother that he had found a spare key that his father had in one of his drawers. She just looked at him and then just grabbed him and started hitting him for the first time with her hands, which then made her end up breaking her nails. Her friend then came and took her off of John, she then told her friend bye to get out of her house.

When her friend had finally left, John's mother started fighting John, telling him that she hated him, and wanted him to die so that he could get out of her life because it all started ever since he was born.

John didn't get mad at her that time even though he was crying because she was crying also so hard, so he was just like go ahead and take it all out on me because he should've told her but he didn't.

John's mother was like, "You knew about it all and you did not tell me." So John said yes, because he thought she would have probably known already, and if he would have told her, he would have gotten a beating by Nicole.

"I would not have cared," his mother said. "I do not care if she would have killed you! You should've told me. Get out my house, get out now because I do not ever want you back in here, pack up your stuff and go!" his mother said to him. So John put some clothes in a bag, and when he was walking out of her house, at his age of eight, his mother called him Satan, telling him to go back to hell and burn in hell.

John went straight to his friend Rick's house, and he told him that his mother had kicked him out.

John stayed there for about a month, not going to school, with Rick's father just trying to be there for him. Rick's father was a Jamaican, so it was not anything new to him. Rick's father said to him every day, "Just don't go back over there and become a killer."

John had missed too much days of school, so the school wanted some information on him. However, John's mother was not answering all the school phone calls, Rick told him. The school was asking all of the friends he knew in school, which were all the bad ones of course.

Sunshine Elementary School then sent someone to John's house to find out where he was and how he was doing. Still no one answered the door and there was a car in front of the house. Therefore, each day there had been reported back to the schoolhouse with no information being given, so then the school took it all to another level.

Rick then came back home from school and told John that he was being searched for by the police now because his mother told them that he ran away from home when they had caught her one day on the street.

Rick's dad then told John that he would have to go back home now because he was not trying to go back in jail anymore, so it was time for him to go, because right now he was making that money and don't want it all to go to an end already.

So Rick and a couple of John's other friends that knew what he was going through, got one of their older brothers to come and pick them up to take John back home, it was about ten of them in one car.

When they had reached John's mother's house, everybody walked him to the door and waited until someone opened up the door. Someone had opened up the door but had walked away not showing his or her face to everyone.

John's friends were then saying that if he needed them they'd be outside for some time, waiting with Claude's older brother to make sure he won't get kicked out again and then walking the streets alone.

CHAPTER 4

John's mother was right there sitting down around the table asking where he was. Therefore, John began saying, "You wanted me out, right? So I left." "Whose house were you sleeping at every night?" John's mother kept asking him, but John was never going to tell her. Therefore, he told her that he was sleeping in boxes and bushes.

"You think this is a joke!" John's mother kept asking him. "Leave me alone," John started telling his mother. Nevertheless, while looking at him with anger, John's mother then said, "Sorry for kicking you out, because it was wrong of me to have done that." But John knew already that it was because of the investigation that his friends had told him about that was going on.

That same night, John's mother cooked him dinner, telling him that she would like to talk to him about what had currently happened. She told him that it was just because she was going through something with his father, and she did not know what to do.

"So you blamed me for it, right?" John asked her. "Yes, who else could I take it all out on?" John's mother asked him.

"However, I am going to try to be a good mother from now on, OK?" "If you say so," John replied to her. "However, you have to work on how you talk to me," his mother told him.

John then just gave her no answer, just a look.

She then looked at him for the first time, even though he knew that there was a reason for it. John's mother told him that she loved him.

John then began feeling so happy deep inside him. "I have never heard her say that before," he said to himself, with a smile on his face, "not even to my father."

John began feeling special and feeling as if he was someone wanted and loved now in life, by his mother.

After a little time of playing cards with John, his mother told him that tomorrow at school some people are going to come and question him about where he was and why. Asking him, "Why did you run away for such a long time? Moreover, where did you go?"

"I want you to tell them that you ran away because you wanted to, OK? Because you wanted to be with your friends and walk the streets all day and night," John's mother told him.

"If they ask you if I beat you, say my mother has never put her hands on me, and if you tell them that, I will give you anything that you want OK, Jonathan?"

That next morning, John's mother dressed him up and told him to make sure that he says everything that she told him to say. When John had gotten to school, the school security immediately told them that they see him walking in school.

They had then sent John straight to the principal's office and started questioning him. Asking him questions like, what has been going on in his life. Had his mother been treating him right? Does she threaten or beat him? "Tell us why did you ran away from your mother at such a young age?" they kept asking him.

However, John just kept telling them what his mother told him to tell them because that would have made her happy with him.

Mrs. Vigness, John's second grade teacher at that time, knew John very well because it was his second year with her as his main elementary school teacher. He had become real close with her and a couple of other teachers at that time, because he used to open up to them and tell them what was really going on in his life.

Because one time, John's girlfriend at that time, told them the truth why he came to school with a black eye, she was like "He's the only one that cannot stay after school to play kickball because he had to rush home to his mother."

Therefore, Mrs. Vigness knew he did not get into any street fight because everyone liked him. Therefore, Mrs. Vigness told him not to let his mother beat him up. However, he still told everyone else another story, like his older brother Clinton beat him up.

Therefore, Mrs. Vigness knew John was lying again, and she asked him why was he lying to the police and administration about it all. Therefore, John told her because he was finally making his mother happy with him, and that she was making him feel good by telling him that she loves him now.

Mrs. Vigness just looked at John and started crying, telling him that he needs to learn how to not make someone play with his young mind. Therefore, she went back to administration and told them that John was lying about it all.

However, when the school called back the school board, John gave them the same answers. Therefore, they had John being watched over and checked on every week until they were able to hear what they've been expecting to hear, to start a case of child neglect on his mother.

At home, John's mother was so happy because she had heard that the case had been finally dropped, which was not, John's mother was just told that it was. John did not really care about it all though because he was happy with the way he was now being treated by his mother.

At school, Mrs. Vigness, John's teacher was just like, "John, you need to open up your mouth and talk before something happens to you again." However, John told her that his mother told him that he will be all right, and that his mother will take care of him, and had told him not to listen to anyone else anymore because she was the one that was feeding him and being there for him more than anyone else.

John's teacher never called his house again with any complaints, even if he got into trouble in school. John had also found out that his mother told the school that she does not want Mrs. Vigness to be his teacher anymore. Nevertheless, John told them no, he does not want to come out of Mrs. Vigness's class.

John's father then moved back to their house, out of nowhere, one day when he had came home from school. John then found out that his mother and father were going out again and having a wonderful time together again with one another.

John's parents then took him for the first time to Universal Studios and Disney World for about four days for the summer, with his father's sisters. So now, everybody was feeling great in life, with everyone at each other's side again.

When John and his family had gone back down to south Florida, he was hoping that it all would stay the same, meaning with them all happy.

As time went John's mother made another best friend, her name was Lori. Lori started to come over John's parents' house every week to be with his mother. John had then gotten to know Lori after a while, and because of her being such a nice and loving churchwoman, John ended up loving Lori so much—she was helping him out with his wrong actions and homework because he was now in third grade, so that he could keep the good treatment that his mother was giving to him.

Lori then introduced John to Monica, her sister, who was also very kind and caring. Then Lori introduced John to their mother Tiffany, who was also a strong and loving woman.

"The school bus is about to arrive, Lori," Monica said. So Lori went and got her nephew Tim. Lori had taken John over to their house one day after school because his mother wanted her to watch him.

They then introduced John to Tim, the one that John ended up calling his best friend because of how much time they began spending together and getting to know one another.

Tim at first seemed like a good boy but then ended up being just as bad as John was. However, Tim did not get beatings for none of his bad actions, just a simple talk saying not to do that because it was wrong.

Tim did not ever really get beatings in life because his auntie Lori would always protect and shield him day and night. Lori was like Tim's bodyguard meaning if you messed with Tim, you have messed with her also.

Lori used to always say that she would be John's bodyguard and shield if his mother ever started beating him again in front of her.

While John would always drink water or Kool-Aid, all Tim would be drinking would be Coca-Cola as if it was water, and it went down so easy for him. That was why he had already started to develop a stomach like his grandfather.

John and Tim used to be together every day after school, spending time with one another all day, and they used to eat all day while watching *Home Alone* parts one and two. John and Tim used to laugh like crazy while watching these movies. John even one time was laughing so hard that the juice that he was drinking ended up coming out of his nose.

John had even ended up wetting the couch one time. And Tim ended up choking on the food that they were eating.

So they ended up not being able to eat or drink anything while watching *Home Alone* movies, which they used to watch back to back, because Lori did not want them to die from choking. Therefore, they ended up having to eat and drink either before or after the movies.

They used to be looking so funny together whenever they went out together. John was looking the most funniest though, Tim had a little bit of brand name clothing, and John only had 100 percent cotton clothing.

Tim used to laugh at John because he had one day, BUFU, which was really supposed to be the brand name FUBU.

They'd both go out with tight pants and shirts on sometimes, and John's briefs were so tight that he had to rip holes in them because they were squeezing little John, and they mostly had on slippers on their feet night and day.

John and Tim did a lot of bad things to others, watching each other cause trouble to another, doing things to other people like the way they had seen it done in all the *Home Alone* movies.

They used to make fun of each other and other people in the mall and spit spitballs from the elevators while they were going up on it.

John and Tim started throwing water balloons at people's cars whenever they would walk on certain streets with a lot of traffic going fast. Then their actions had gotten even worse because they started throwing rocks at people's car windows as each car passed by fast, first one to break a window made the decisions where and what they are going to eat that night.

However, before any decisions were made, they always had to make sure that whenever they broke someone's car window that they run for their lives so that they would not get into any trouble. Eventually they were caught and punished, well, really John, because his mother also had to put money in to fix someone's car window.

Therefore, John began getting different babysitters, mainly his mother's friends, on the weekends. One was Tonya. Tonya, John's mother's friend, a thirty-something-year-old woman, was watching over him for about a week because he heard his mother and father were going somewhere to celebrate their honeymoon. John did not really know her so he stayed in his room most of the time because that was where his babysitter wanted to babysit him, in his parents' house not hers.

John had brought a pornographic tape over from Tim's house since his mother was not going to be around. Therefore, he felt no one was really going to be bothering him, so he closed his door and began watching it.

John had forgot to lock the door though so now when his mother's friend Tonya came in and saw John watching it, she was like "John, tell me what do you know at such a young age about sex?" and then asked him if he was still a virgin at the age of nine and about to go on ten.

John told her that he had watched his cousins and had tried it before with some girls in Jamaica, and that his teacher even taught him how to have sex.

Tonya was like "Prove it to me," so John was like "No," because she was going to go back and tell his mother, so Tonya said, "No, I would not tell anybody, I promise."

Therefore, Tonya told John to take off his clothes and then she will, after him. Tonya was a little big so he didn't know what to say to her because he did not know if he could or not, but surprisingly, he tried. All Tonya said to him in the end was come back to her when it grows because John can't do anything for a woman like her, right now. Therefore, Tonya was John's fifth sex experiment, which he had failed.

Tonya had told John's mother what happened while she was babysitting when she had came back, and John did not know.

Therefore, his mother was like, "Do not be bringing any small little girls in my house because I heard you were over here already having sex in my house with one of my friends that was not even your age." John's mother told John that her friend told her that John pushed her on the bed and started having sex with her "against her will."

Therefore, John's mother told John that he was going to grow up raping girls because he was already raping grown women.

However, the one thing that she did not know was that every woman that John had tried to have sex with were older and wanted him to try to, without him even having to ask for sex, and they all were older Jamaican women, and her friend was one. However, the reason why she wanted to do it was that she could not find a man.

"Anyway, what do you know about sex?" John's mother asked him.

John's mother began wondering in her mind and then said, "So you are not a virgin anymore, Jonathan?" Then John asked her what a virgin is. "Never mind," his mother said, John's mother then told him to come to her and have sex with her like how her friend told her he did.

So now in John's head he was like "Are not you my mother?" Therefore, he began believing his grandmother lied to him by telling that she was the one that gave birth to him.

John then told his mother that he could not because he does not want his grandmother to come for him because of what she used to do whenever she saw him touching on an older lady in certain, so he began thinking that she was trying to trick him.

"I am your mother, and what I say goes," John's mother said, "and it is not what your grandmother says, it is what I say." She even took off her clothes and put it on the floor, and that was when John truly felt that she was just another woman, not his mother.

John then began getting confused, asking himself, "Who is this woman really, and why does she want to have sex with me, while she has a husband?"

John just then wondered off, wondering who she was, his mother, or his grandmother's friend? After some time, he went back to her and told her that she was not his mother.

"So tell me, who are you? Really, I want to know," John kept asking her, saying, "Truly, if you were my mother, you would not have treated me the way you did when we had first met and trying to kill me. I should have listened to Mrs. Vigness and had gotten you locked up."

John's mother then just looked at him and started crying, telling him to get away from her, and then locked herself in her room.

Then John called Tonya and asked her why she told his mother that he raped her. Tonya told John that it was because she could get in trouble for having sex with a young child like him, so she had to protect herself by making up a lie, just in case he goes out and tells his friends about it and then the police come looking for her.

"Therefore, you lied to me, Tonya," John's mother said out of nowhere. She had picked up the phone in her room and was listening to John talk to Tonya. However, John did know his mother was listening but still Tonya then told John that she was going to get him back for that.

John's mother then told Tonya that John did not know that she was on the phone listening to whom he was calling because John had already known that he was not allowed to use their phone. "Get off the phone," John's mother then told John, "because I am going to talk to Tonya."

Ever since that day John did not see Tonya come back over to his mother's house, and his mother had told him that she was not mad because she allowed him to have sex with her. It was the whole fact of John's mother believing and trusting in her, and now she cannot anymore because of such a small situation that had went down that was not anything.

CHAPTER 5

"John, pack up and get ready. We are going back to Jamaica," his mother said to him out of nowhere one day. John was so happy. Then when he got there, everyone was just looking at him sad. While he had a smile on his face, all day and night asking for his grandfather.

John had found out that they did not want to tell him something from one of his older cousins. When he had finally reached his grandmother and grandfather's house, John then said hello to his grandmother, and she gave John a hug hello, asking him, "How have you been in America, Johnny?"

Her hug was tight and long as if she did not want to let John go. Why, John did not know. He went outside continuously looking for his grandfather and never found him. John saw his car parked, so John was like he must be inside the house or around the house hiding from him.

John's grandfather was not in there when John had checked around the house and nobody would tell him where John's grandfather was whenever he asked someone about his grandfather.

They woke John up early on Saturday, and his grandmother bathed him like how she used to when he was younger. While she was bathing John, he had asked her why she lied to him and told him that he was going to go and live with his mother. John's grandmother told John, "She is your mother, and do not think she is not, because she is." John was like, "No, she is not."

Then John's grandmother told him to believe her and no one else because "she is his mother, it is just you'll are not close to each other because you grew up with us, your grandparents."

Then John's grandmother put some church clothes on him and told him not to go outside until she is ready to go. John did not ask another person after that conversation with his grandmother.

She then finally had gotten ready, and a ride was outside waiting for them. John could not believe it, he was about to have his first limo ride. They were all dressed up as if they were going to church in their own private limo.

They then reached a church and it was the biggest church John had ever gone to so far in Jamaica. The church had an enormous amount of family and friends in there only, and they all one by one were just hugging John, crying, saying, "Your grandfather will always and forever love and be here for you, Johnny." "I already know that," with a big smile on his face, John told him.

"Where is my grandfather? I want to see him now," John began telling them. That is when they all found out that John did not know that his grandfather had passed away and that he was here now at his grandfather's funeral.

John then saw a casket being brought into the church, and while everyone stood up, even his great-grandmother stood with help. John was then told to stand also, but he then ended up sitting down before anyone else, John then saw a church service paper on the bench. John picked it up to start drawing on it. Then he saw his grandfather face on it so he started laughing at his grandfather because of how he was looking in the picture.

John was in the third grade at that time. Therefore, he was able to read a brief description about the kind of man his grandfather was, and that he would be missed because he was loved by many friends and family.

John then read RIP, his grandfather's name, "Doctor," the day, month, and year he was born, to this year; and the date looked like a couple of days ago before he had came back to Jamaica.

John still did not understand what was really going on because he saw no one praising and singing to our Father God. Services started with a song with calm praises and thanks to our Father.

"Come, brethren. It is time for our last words to our good brother that believed in Christ our Father and God our Creator. Our brother is now with him in heaven, living a better and more loving life."

They then opened up the casket, and John just began looking at the casket not knowing who was in there. John was told not to get up and go over by the casket but that was where everyone else was going so of course he was going to want to go, with or without permission.

John then was just drawing on his grandfather's face and laughing at him because he gave him a beard like Santa Claus. He could not get up yet and walk over there because his grandmother was just watching him.

John had fallen asleep after a while because he was feeling lonely and bored. However, his grandmother was keeping a close eye on him still. John was then put into the limo again, and he thought he was being brought back home.

Nevertheless, he ended up going to one of his grandfather's family house, on the side of it though and it was then they buried the casket along side of that same house he was at and covered it in the ground with dirt.

John, his family, and friends then ended up having some goat soup, and everybody was talking alongside one another. John began looking at his grandfather's car, with no one telling him, where his grandfather was.

John and his mother then returned to America. Lori went and picked them up. Lori then started asking John how was his grandfather's funeral when she picked them up from the airport, and if John was going to miss his grandfather.

John did not answer her because he still had no understanding of it all.

John went straight to Lori when he and his mother had been picked up, and was there waiting for Tim to come home from school. Therefore, he went looking for a movie that he had never seen before. John had ended up finding a movie called *Ghost*. When he had seen the movie stacked up, he started thinking about *Ghostbusters,* so he watched it.

However, to understand that movie, he had watched that movie about three times. He had finally understood it at the end of the third time why the woman was crying so much and it was because her husband had died. At first, John was laughing at her.

When she was dreaming about her husband, all night and day, and he was right there beside her.

It was then John had gotten the understanding of what happened to his grandfather, the one he loved the most in his life because he was John's angel right here on earth and he felt his grandfather's shoulder was the shoulder he could have cried on, all day and all night.

John ended up questioning himself night and day about it all, but never asked anyone how he had died. He then thought about the letters that he had seen above his grandfather's head, which were RIP. "No, he is not dead, and I am stupid for saying that," John kept telling himself every night as he sneaked and watched the movie *Ghost* when he had reached back home.

John still never really understood what it meant so when he began going back to school he was very quiet because he had so much on his mind, mainly about if his grandfather really died.

John then asked his teacher Mrs. Vigness what RIP means. Mrs. Vigness told him that it is a short way to say rest in peace to a person.

"Who died, Jonathan?" She kept continuously asking John.

She even ended up asking the woman she did not like at all, his mother, and his mother told her nothing.

When Tim had come over by John's house that same day, John asked him what does RIP means and he said rest in peace.

However, John still was like "What does that mean?" and Tim said when someone dies, people then tell them to RIP, telling them to rest in peace in heaven.

Then Tim was like, "Let's go and play the video games," but John was like, "No, I do not feel like it." So then Tim was like "Let's go and play outside," but John was like, "I want to be left alone," so Tim was like, "All right."

John then started calling himself dumb and had then started crying because he had took so long to understand really what happened to his grandfather. John was like, "How could he have died though?"

John had then thought about it all after a while, wondering how and why.

John had then started blaming himself, telling himself that if he had not left his grandfather by himself, he would have been all right, but he left him. Therefore, he felt that it was all his fault.

John kept talking to himself, saying he finally found out why his grandfather was not there, and why nobody was happy with him being there, with him or her, when he had went back to Jamaica.

John began lying on his bed thinking about it all every night, with no one with him, helping him to understand why his grandfather passed away.

He kept blaming himself and thinking about his grandfather, night and day. John even started crying at night, with his head underneath his pillow.

John kept holding in a lot and crying so much at night while he was supposed to be sleeping, that one day he went to school with his eyes red, thinking about his grandfather, crying, and walking still with his grandfather's picture in his hand.

Mrs. Vigness did not know what was wrong with him. Therefore, she called John's mother to come and pick him up. Nevertheless, she always made up a lie and said either she was working or not around to pick John up. Therefore, Mrs. Vigness started to keep him close to her and always telling him that everything will be all right because she was right there for him, whenever he was ready to speak.

John cried each and every night before he fell asleep while during the day he would be treated so unkindly by his mother, with beatings and real abuse because the school was calling her too much and asking her too much questions about her son.

John was no longer getting into trouble at school now though because he became a quiet student.

Mrs. Vigness, John's number one teacher knew that there was something wrong with him. Therefore, Mrs. Vigness started to drop her class off at the cafeteria for lunchtime and she would ask John to get his lunch first, and then come back with her to class. So that she could talk to John and try to help him.

John was known as a loud troublemaker, a mean face little boy, not a quiet, sad-looking young boy with tears coming down his eyes.

The school administration was asking what's wrong with him also because they missed John in their office corner.

Mrs. Vigness kept on taking John back to class with her for lunch together for the rest of that school year, talking to him and asking him what was truly wrong with him. However, John never ended up telling her whom he lost in his life.

John would not even tell her anything because that was one problem John truly had in life, he would not talk to anyone other than his grandfather, the one that he felt truly loved him.

Therefore, John held in all his depression and anger from everybody in his young age, and it was all mainly because of his mother.

Mrs. Vigness told John's guidance counselor about John's mind and actions now in class, right in front of John when they came in class to get him.

"He is looking lost now," she told them, and she already knew that there was not anyone bothering him or picking on him in school. Therefore, it had to be someone at his home.

"It had to be somebody or something in his life every day," she mentioned, "but he just seems too scared to say if it was his mother, father, grandmother, or grandfather. Therefore, "you know we have to contact child abuse because it seems like no one else could help him, with whatever he is going through right now in his early childhood."

Mrs. Vigness never noticed but some of the counselors did that when she had mentioned John's grandfather, John had started crying and went inside of Mrs. Vigness closet and closed it for the rest of that school day.

Mrs. Vigness then took John home because she could not reach his mother by phone. John's mother had then locked herself in the room when she had seen Mrs. Vigness coming up to her door and turned off her television and phone until the teacher left. She then just told John to go inside and tell her tomorrow if his mother says or do anything to him.

John's mother then told him, "Do not ever come home and bring her to my house." However, John's teacher kept on dropping him off since he never told her that his mother was beating him because of Mrs. Vigness coming to her house.

One day, John's mother saw him crying in his room, so she asked John what was it he was crying for. "Did you hurt yourself?" she asked him. John said, no.

"Hold up, are you crying because your grandfather died?" John's mother then said to him. "No, I know you are not crying because he is dead. Why should you anyways?" John's mother asked John. "He never loved you or wanted you. If he did he would not have sent you here to live with me. Your grandfather hated you, Jonathan. Do not think that he loved you." John's mother kept telling him.

The one reason why John did not believe her was because John's grandfather had called for him before he had passed away. John wanted to talk to him, and John's mother would not let him because she wanted John's grandfather, who was her father, to give all his love and attention to her because her relationship with John's grandfather was different from theirs, when she was younger. Therefore, John's mother was jealous of all the love and wanting for John, that his grandfather was giving him and not her.

John's mother then looked at him calmly, thinking, and then began telling John that if it were not for him stressing his grandfather, his grandfather would have lived a longer life. Therefore, he is dead and gone now, and he is never coming back and it was John's entire fault.

"So do not expect to see him again anytime soon, at least not until you're dead and gone which I'm hoping will be soon," John's mother then said to him.

"As a matter of fact here, let me give you something to cry for because you are crying for foolishness right now," she then said to him.

John's mother then began beating him and telling him to get his grandfather out of his head. That day just made John madder and sadder deeply inside because his mother was beating him for loving and missing his grandfather.

She knew John hated cold water, so she would force him to take off all his clothes and then put him in the shower with cold water running.

Nevertheless, after a while—like an hour and a half—John got used to it. She then one day got one of those pancake flippers, and told him to stretch out his hands, and then just started to beat him with it.

John then cried all night in his dark closet that night, wrapping himself up with his own arms.

The next morning, he started having headaches and getting very dizzy, it caused him to see whatever was in front of him to move around, and he was feeling like he was about to drop. John would hold his head up crying because of the pain and feeling in his head that he began to have.

When John went to school and kept walking as if he was about to drop, the school began worrying about him and wanting to help him. They sat John down in the office, and went into a meeting about what they were going to do about this problem. When they had come back out the office to talk to John, he was on the floor with his hands over his eyes because he was seeing everything moving around and tilting in his sight.

The school then sent their office administrators to his house, with him in the car, waiting there until his mother finally came back home. When they had gotten there, her car was not there, and John was in the car crying because he already knew that when they would leave him there, he was going to get a beating.

"Where is your father?" they asked him, so John told them that he was never home, so it was as if he does not really live there anymore, and if he were home, he would not help him anymore, anyways. Therefore, they just walked him in the house, but they could not go inside so they just left him there, telling him that if he starts to get dizzy again, to call 911.

John finally came home one day when they were still there because many times, his mother would not even come home until they had left. Then she would beat him and tell him to stop bringing them to her house and causing stress in her life. She had already told him that when Mrs. Vigness kept coming to the house.

John's mother just kept on beating him because he was stressing her by bringing those people to her house repeatedly. So one day, when she had already a bad day doing something, and saw a policeman standing outside of her house. Watching it and then telling her that she needs to start taking care of her child before charges are filed against her.

That day, after the officer left, John's mother threw him down on the floor telling him to get out of her life before she kills him because he was never going to put his hands on her again. John's mother then ran into the kitchen, with tears in her eyes, and picked up a kitchen knife she then threw at John. However, she had missed the first time so John got up and had started to run to his room.

John's mother then went back for the knife; then calling John by another name, she threw it at him again. John's mother could have gotten him with it, but he had closed the door just in time and locked it.

He then fell on his room floor with his heart beating hard. Then had gotten back up, and ran into his closet, shivering and wondering if his mother was about to come and kill him.

John then came out of his room when he thought she had left the house, but she did not and he thought she did because John heard her grab her keys and opened the front door then closed it.

As soon as he went to the kitchen to get a piece of paper towel to wipe his eyes and blow his nose, John's mother then came out from inside of the laundry room, where she was hiding with a knife.

John's mother then grabbed him and put the knife to his neck, telling him that he had put his hands on the wrong person, and now he was going to die.

John was then like, "I did not touch you or do anything to you, why do you want to kill me so badly."

John's mother began looking into his eyes saying, "Because—" She then stopped and was there looking in his eyes for about three minutes, looking as if she was serious, and wanting to kill him like how she wanted to fight Nicole for doing things with her husband, so it was a look with meaning.

"I hate you, and I want you to die, I want you to go to prison, and be locked up for life." "Who is . . . ?" John then asked her.

John's mother then told him to go in the kitchen, and wash the dishes now and to tell her when he was finished. After John had finished washing the dishes, he went to his mother to tell her that he was finished.

However, when John went in her room to tell her, she was crying. When she saw him, she rushed at him with one of her high-heeled shoes and started hitting him. John then dropped down on the floor because he was in some serious pain now.

John's mother then kept on telling John to get up, but he could not because of all the pain he was in. So she dragged him into the laundry room and turned off all the lights and then locked the door.

All John saw was a blinking red light when he finally picked up his head—he had been hit on it, too. He was holding his head, but mainly feeling pain in his back, legs, arms, and feet.

John looked around after about four hours since he had been in there. John could not even move because every move caused more aching pain.

Late that night, John's mother opened up the door and told him to go to bed.

John did not even go to school the next day because of all the pain that he was still in and not being able to walk, just hop.

She then told him to get out of his bed that morning, and to get dress because he was staying with her all day that day. "I do not want you going back telling anyone that I had hit you, all right," she told John.

That same day, the police called John's mother on her cell phone and began talking to her, asking her why John was not in school that day. She told the officers that had her on speaker that John was not feeling good today so John was with her today so that she can take care of him.

They told her that she needs to start being a loving mother toward him, so that means helping him while he went through his deep depression and anxiety in his life now because he was a young child.

"Put John on the phone so that we can talk to him," they told her. The police asked John if he was all right and if his mother was treating him bad. John looked at her first, "I am all right and having fun with my mother," John told them.

It was more than one, it sounded like so they told John to make sure to go to school on Monday. It was Friday and the weekend was coming up.

"Jonathan," one officer said, "we are all going to be there waiting for you, OK?" They already knew that his mother was telling him to say all of what he had said to them.

When John and his mother had gotten back home, she began hitting him and telling him that if she ever was locked up in jail because of him, she was going to come back and find him, and kill him.

So now at night, John was not only scared of his mother killing him, but also his grandfather coming back for him because John was not there for him when his grandfather needed him. Therefore, John felt that his grandfather's death was his entire fault.

John ended up not sleeping for that whole weekend because of so many thoughts and all the visions that he was seeing while he was lying down at night by himself.

Then it all finally had an end one Sunday night, John began getting dizzy and began having visions in his mind of the past.

Finally, John had gotten some sleep but he had then had his first seizure.

Monday morning came and he was shaking, he had bit his tongue somehow last night, and had now waken up on the floor. John had so many things going through his mind that when he left the house and was walking to school to meet the officers, John passed out, and had a seizure attack on the sidewalk.

John awoke in the hospital. He had a couple of seizures, one witness was a woman, John collapsed in front of her house.

John then passed out again and started shaking again. John ended up staying in the hospital for a couple days, but then released too fast because his mother did not want him in there. However, before John left, the doctors asked John what was stressing him out so much because he was such a young child, with no bills or wife.

The doctors put John on medication since he would not talk. It was medication for stress and depression because that was what caused him to pass out and have those seizures.

John's mother got mad at him for the hospital bills that she had to pay the doctors because John did not have any insurance under his name since he had come from Jamaica.

He did not know that he had no insurance under his name, "Anyway, what is insurance?" John then asked his mother.

She was like since John gave her work to do, she was now going to give him more work to do in return.

John's mother had then forgotten that the police wanted to talk to John because she did not even call the school and told the school what had happened to John that day.

Therefore, they had ended up calling the Florida Department of Children and Families again and started up another case against her. They went to the house to talk to John about what was going on now in his life, and John had told them that he had passed out on the road while he was going to meet the police and what the doctors said to him about his condition.

That was when John's mother started having meetings with the county and a big chance of being arrested for child abuse and neglect because John's mother did not come right away to the hospital anyway when she found out about John's situation.

Children and Families found that out when they went to the hospital to ask questions.

Children and Families said then that if it was not for John's father also being in the house with them, they would have taken John away from her and she would have been arrested.

Children and Families kept checking up on John day after day to make sure that he was feeling comfortable in the house with his mother. John could not tell them anything or else he would have been killed. That was what his mother told him before they got there.

John kept locking himself in his closet crying, thinking about his grandfather and that he was going to die after every threat she made toward him.

John was feeling unloved, unwanted and felt as if he was about to be killed soon.

After a while of being on medication, John had began feeling relaxed. It had taken him a while, but he had gotten over his grandfather's death a little bit. He was not seeing him anymore at nighttime like how he used to.

However, John was still wishing his grandfather was right there with him.

When John went back to school, the school administrators checked up on him every day and also the Children and Families Department did so every Wednesday. John then had gotten back to his normal self again but now feeling empty with no one there for him.

Lori then reminded John that he would always have a father in heaven watching over him. Who will always be watching over him always and forever, and even before he was born, Jesus Christ was the one growing him in his mother's stomach.

Lori then said, "John, your grandfather is in a better place right now, where he wants to be and he is watching over you alongside our Father God. So please be happy, baby."

CHAPTER 6

Lori was one woman that John thanked God for bringing into his life, thankful for because she helped bring a little knowledge, wisdom, and understanding into his life. John would say that she was one of the best people who have helped and inspired him to stay strong, and do right in his young life. John even then began thinking that Lori was his real mother because of how much attention and talk she was giving to him.

John began to thank God for bringing Lori in his life—continuously with a smile on his face. Lori helped bring God into his life by bringing him and Tim to church every Saturday and then on Sunday nights, teaching them more and more about their Father.

John had believed in his Father God from when he was growing up in Jamaica, but he never was really into it or fully understanding it because he was so young.

John and Tim used to fast and pray with Tonya and then study the Bible. Well, actually just read verses, night after night, because John was not much of a reader growing up. Tim was not either but he knew more than John did, though.

John began actually to change his mind about something he was going to do because of all the anger that had built in him.

However, so many arguments between John and his mother continued and expressions that John did not like so it all just made John end up staying the same.

However, he still had faith in his Father, that he was watching over him night and day.

John started wanting to play around so much now in school, but he would not get any referrals because the school was so happy to see him happy in life again.

John kept being checked on every week by Children and Families, and the school administrators.

He then started acting as if he never knew what was going on in his life because he was always smiling, laughing, and making fun of people again. It was as if he was spoiled at home and could do whatever he wanted to do and not get into any trouble.

Because of actions and jokes that he was giving about everyone, the school gave John his nickname Dumbo because he had big ears. It was one of his elective teachers who first started calling him that name because he used to crack jokes on her about how she looked more like the instrument's cleaner, not its player.

However, he had one teacher that he loved so much, Ms. Brown, but John still made fun of her saying she could have made an imitation of the movie *Beauty and the Beast* called "Beastliest Women and the Man."

Ms. Brown had gotten so mad at him after he had said that, that she made him go in the corner, putting the board eraser on his head, and standing in the corner, holding one leg up, with both eyes closed as the class spitted spitballs at him, and threw paper balls at him.

Ms. Brown began laughing at him, and continued laughing at him for the rest of the day, and not assigning any more class work for the rest of that class.

John was then like, "You'll think this is real funny, right." Ms. Brown then asked John if he learned his lesson about making fun of her. Therefore, John was like "Yes, beast."

John had continued not getting any referrals from his teachers in school, only administrators, like whenever they saw him coming out of the line and cutting people in line in the cafeteria.

As John began getting happier, his mother got meaner and seemed to be starting to feel more uncomfortable with him around her. She was looking at him differently with a look of jealousy as if he was getting more money or he reminded her of someone that she did not like.

John began thinking again that it was because his grandfather had loved him more so she had gotten very jealous.

John's mother was always strict with him about everything, but it seems like because of so much happiness he was getting from everyone, she began beating him every day again, knowing he could easily get her locked up.

John's mother just used to make up lies to beat him, telling him that she hated him because of all that he had put her through in life with the police, her friends, and her family.

She started dropping her purse or jacket at the front door whenever she came home, and if John did not pick them up for her as soon as possible, he would get a beating for being lazy.

John tried talking to her friends about it all, but each time he said something, they would just go back to his mother about it, and she would just be like, "Don't believe anything that comes out of Jonathan's mouth because he's a bald-faced liar about everything."

John could not eat anything from his mother's house without her permission, and she was hardly home. She would not even pick up her cell phone whenever he came home and John wanted something to eat. According to her, John was eating up all the food, but she used to eat much more than he did.

John even used to take extra food from school out the cafeteria to take home to eat at night because he would get the blame when all the food was gone in the house.

The only time he was able to eat was whenever he went to school or on the weekends whenever he went to Tim's house because John's father was never home so he was always on his own in that house.

Lori would just feed John and Tim like they were wild animals and then at nighttime, she would take them to an all-you-can-eat buffet restaurant so that they could eat like wild animals.

However, during the weekdays and coming back home from school, John would have been just getting madder about it all, but just hold it all in and not telling any of her friends because it was not making any difference for him.

John started saying, "forget her" each time he felt unwanted and mistreated, "I don't need her, and she does not need me so forget her."

John started talking to himself about the things that were troubling him, and that was just making him worse in his mind and life.

John did not even want to be alive anymore, and he was only about twelve years old. He did not understand why, whenever it came down to him, his mother's word was bigger than his father's word, whenever he would come around to help him.

Night after night, John's mother kept on getting him madder, with John not knowing if she had realized that she was just getting him madder and aggressive in his mind and life.

She had then begun to make John feel like he could handle anything or anyone she could throw at him now because he had now survived so many nights of brutal beatings with no purpose and with no meaning to them, so that he could learn not to do wrong, but really because she wanted him to die.

John would wake up and go to school happy, and have fun because whenever he would go into school, he felt that school was his Chuck E. Cheese. Therefore, all he began doing were just jokes and pranks on all the administrators mainly and teachers.

John began getting salutes as if he was their sergeant or colonel because his father used to always cut his hair on the weekends whenever he was there.

John's mother never wanted to take him to the barbershop and spend money on him, his father did not want to either, so his hair was always messed up.

His tapeline was like in the middle of his head, so they began saluting John, but in the middle of their heads.

Teachers were calling him Dumbo, and the bottom of his shoes would be coming off because he only got one pair of shoes from Payless every school year.

John was also known as an all-week-same-clothes "young soldier," because he never really had clothing, and he only had about four pairs of briefs, and he would only be able to wash once every two weeks or else they would complain about their water bill repeatedly.

Tim had then given John some of his briefs, but in order for John to have worn them, he had to pin them up, each time. So that they would not drop off of him because Tim was bigger than him, but the same age.

Each pair of his own briefs had holes in them that he had cut because again they were hurting little John especially when he would have to run home from school.

John had thirty minutes to walk, a long way home each day. It was a good thing though that he had grown up in Jamaica. So he was used to walking the long walks, but it was easier in Florida because there were no hills to climb, and he had shoes on his feet that were taped up, so even when the sun was hot, his feet were not burning because of the hot road. John always went home wet, looking like it was raining outside because he sweated so easily.

John would come home to do his homework, wash the dishes, sweep the floor, mop, clean her room, bed, and closet, and sweep the outside porch.

He did so many things in that house on his own, and every time his mother's friends came over they would be like, "You keep your home so clean, girl." All she would say was that she had to because she had to keep her man happy at all times, after his long hours of work in the dirt, and John always thought that she was working, but she never used to work.

His mother only spent money and ate food. Then she spent most of her time going out with her friends. One funny thing she used to say was that she needed to get back into shape, and then tell her husband to buy her a workout machine and whenever he had bought one, she would use it only the first couple of days then it would be John's play toy because she would never go back on it, and it was also used for decoration to impress the crowd that would go in their house at times.

Whenever his mother's friends came over, "I'm working on my body shape for my man," she used to say, but still never used it. John's mother used to spend her man's money on things to show off. His mother loved to spend money—well, his father's money—and eat food.

John used to cut the grass every two weeks, wash the cars, and fold up the clothes after he did the laundry, and all she would do was cook once or twice a week, if she knew a friend was coming over.

One weekend, John went to Tim's house to spend that weekend with him because he had not gone there for about a month.

However, when he went back home, nothing had been cleaned for the whole weekend. There were a lot of used forks, spoons, plates, and pots, and pans. Dirty clothes that needed to be washed that same night, especially his father's work clothes.

John had never stayed up so late before since he had started sleeping in his parent home. John had begun washing the clothes and the dishes, taking out all the garbage that was stacked up on the countertops. It was as if they had a get-together with friends and family that night before he had gotten home.

When John was finished washing the dishes, his hands were soaked, and he still was not finished. He had to sweep, mop, and dust, and then last came the garbage, John had to take it all outside at the side of the house with all the frogs outside.

John used to hate going around frogs, he was afraid of frogs because of one time seeing a friend who used to love to play with frogs, catch warts. When he had come back in, he had just left all the clothes in the washer and dryer for another day. But when his father had woken up and needed clothes, he went to John and asked him for it, so John had to take it all out of the dryer and put his work shirts inside of the dryer to dry, so that day his father went to work late because he did not dry all of his clothing. However, John's father never told his mother about the situation when she woke up, so he was all right.

John's mother kept on doing that every weekend that he went to someone's house, but he did not care because he still kept on going, he was having so much fun out of the house and away from her.

"All you need to do now in the house is just cook dinner,' John's mother told him one night, when she was hungry and did not have any money to buy fast food.

Because John was cooking breakfast in the mornings for them when there was no school and he could not go by one of his mother's friends' house.

Surprisingly one day when John came home from school, his grandmother, auntie, and cousin came up from Jamaica, and he did not know that they were coming or even had their papers.

Every day his mother said, "Oh, he's so spoiled. John does not have to do anything in this house." Because she does all the work, then she would end it with "I wish I was able to grow up like how my son is growing up right now, when I was young in Jamaica."

John's mother never even used to beat him unless they went somewhere with another friend. She only threatened him whenever they were not looking at John. She would say, "You lucky they here right now," and that if he would ever open up his mouth about her beating him, she was going to beat the hell out of him when they leave, and go back to Jamaica.

After, John's mother and father had his now two brothers when he was in middle school, John was so happy for them but afraid that they were going to get beatings like him. One was named George and the other Alexander but they did not have the same last name as him.

They ended up being only two years and a couple of months apart from each other's births, and they had no features like John. However, all John really knew was that they came out of his mother's stomach because he saw it when it kept getting bigger.

John's mother began letting John be like the mother really because he was feeding and changing every dirty diaper there was whenever he was home and then putting them to sleep.

She began wanting to lose weight again. Therefore, John's mother began trying to exercise on a day-to-day basis. So he began trying to help her by walking with her at night when his father began taking care of his two sons.

John was trying to suck up to her as much as he could for less beatings, and that was the only time he would actually see her smile in his face, even when he was down and mad at her still in the inside.

Two years later, John began cooking breakfast for them, every Saturday and Sunday in the morning before he went to church, and he would have to bring it in their room with a personalized tray table for each of them with drinks and anything else that they needed or wanted. Since they gave him what he had been wanting so badly.

John felt that he had to make them feel good, especially her because she was a queen in her husband's castle, his mother had begun saying to him.

John even had to start giving her a pedicure and manicure, then scrub the bottom of her feet, and then help her wash her hair, and perm it, as if he was her daughter or something. His mother was like, "Do not get mad because now that he knows how to do it, he can do it for his wife when he grows up."

Therefore, John's wife will not have to go to a hair salon and spend all of his money that he would be working for on a hair design.

His mother then decided to follow a friend's advice to lose weight faster by taking some kind of drug that her friend was able to get because she worked at a hospital. The drug ended up putting her in the hospital for some time. Therefore, John's father had him taking care of his baby brothers.

John's mother then came out, and she had finally lost the weight that she wanted to lose. However, fights began between his mother and father about what she did and every time after a fight, she came and took it all out on him.

Telling John that she hated him and saying that if he were not in her life, she would not be going through all of this pain. So now, his mother wanted him out again because she does not want to lose her husband.

John told her one that, "He wasn't the one that told her to have sex with his father." Moreover, she just looked at John, wanting to say something but never did.

Then his father begun getting very serious with her because he was going through some money problems now, and she was not even there to help him.

John's father told his mother that she was lazy and had two kids to feed and that she could not have even provide for them if it was not for him. Repeatedly, he then begun saying to John's mother, "You follow your friends too much, and you need to find a job, to start becoming a responsible parent in life, now.

That night, she went to John after their fight, with no one around, and told him repeatedly that she hated him and was looking at him like an enemy in her life again.

She was looking at him very hard as if he was the reason for her life's trials.

She then told him to get up and take off all his clothes, and to lie down on his stomach on the bed. She then left his room and then came back after about thirty minutes or longer.

"I am not able to take this anymore in my life," she continuously said, she started to beat him for some reason because she was not saying anything while he was crying.

John turned around, and looked at her, and asked her, "Why are you hitting me?"

She looked at him closely, and then just pushed his head back down, and said, "I hate you!"

"I have wanted you dead and to go back to the pits of hell that you came from," she said, saying not John's name but some other man's name, repeatedly.

John's mother after about an hour left and went back in her room crying, with her husband waiting in there for her.

That night, John had woken up with his mother standing over him with a kitchen knife, wanting to kill him, John then began shaking, but she then left because her husband came to the door and was looking at her.

John could not sleep afterward, he was crying and shaking not because he was scared it was more because he was feeling unloved. "Forget my life," he then said to himself.

Therefore, he then went into the kitchen and took up the kitchen knife off the countertop, and begun pressing it on his throat hard, so hard that if he had moved it, he would have cut his throat, and started bleeding.

After hours of asking God what he was put on this earth for, and not even being loved by his own mother, "Why am I here?" he kept asking his Father

God. He asked his Father God who had ever truly loved him since he was born.

John then thought of his grandfather, and started saying, "I am coming to get your love back," but he then remembered about his brothers. Therefore, he had immediately taken the kitchen knife off of his throat, but was holding it still with a lot of anger in him.

He then thought about his mother, so he had then gone to her door, peeking in to see what side of the bed she was lying on. John was going to kill her, he had it in him not caring if he went to hell or not because she was going to kill him, but then his brother had woken up to use the bathroom and was just looking at him, asking John if he could use the bathroom.

Therefore, John told him yes and took him in the bathroom to use it, and had asked him if he needed or wanted anything else. His brother George then said, "No, however what, was he doing up"?

John had then closed his brothers' room door because his little brother kept asking him questions about what was he doing. John's mother had then woken up and he did not know it when he had went back into the bathroom looking at himself in the mirror with the knife in his hand.

She had then came out the bathroom and had seen him with it, holding the knife to his throat, and all she did was quickly closed the door slightly, and looking as if she wanted him to do it because she did not even tell him not to do it.

Looking at himself in the mirror for sometime wanting to kill himself, John asked himself, "Who was that person that his mother was talking about?" He kept asking himself all night while he was looking at himself in the mirror.

"I want to know," John told himself in the mirror, so he now had a mission to accomplish, and that was to find out just who this man was.

"Is it my grandfather's real name," he asked himself because he had never heard his grandfather's real name before.

Because his grandfather was only called by his nickname, and his nickname was Doctor. However, that name was not the only name on that paper at his funeral. "I do not even remember the name on it," he told himself.

John then wiped his tears and told himself in the mirror that he was going to find out who that person was that his mother was talking about.

When John had walked out the door, she quickly closed back her room door, so he then was like "Dang! I did not even know that she was watching and listening to me."

John then went inside his room and started looking for his grandfather's funeral paper which he had saved. However, when he found it, he had seen a different name on it, not the same name that his mother been calling him since he had his first beating from her.

John began lying on his bed that night, thinking and crying, asking why he was going through such a rough life. Was it too perfect in Jamaica? He had asked his Father in heaven. Moreover, why was he wanted dead, already?

In his first year of middle school, John already knew that no one lives a perfect life, rich or poor, weak or strong; no one lives a perfect life.

John's mother continuously started to come in his room, night after night, in the middle of the night, hitting him and addressing him by that same name.

She continuously put knives over him, looking at him fiercely, saying, "You are going to die . . . !"

Nights of brutal beatings, time after time John had kept on having and experiencing at an early age.

Why, though? He kept on asking himself, and for what reasons. She would never say a word, from time to time.

John's mother would not even allow him to go by his so-called father's mother's home because all his so-called father would do was just leave him at his mother's house after hearing and seeing what he had to go through day after day. Unless John had to go to school the next day, he was trying to be brought anywhere.

John's mother started hitting him with everything in sight that she could get her hands on: from a wooden broomstick that ended up breaking on his back after about three hits. A high-heeled shoe that he had to grab out of her hands and then throw away because it felt like it was about to go through him if she would of continued hitting him with it.

Coming home from school, he would sometimes be about ten minutes late from the time she said he had to be home, which was fifteen minutes after school had let out. She would be like "why are you getting in so late?" John would say, "I left right after school, I do not know why."

She would then beat him, telling him to go inside his room. Asking him why he never listens to her. Coming out of his room, John's mother saw a knife in front of her, the knife she had left in the dining room, just in case John would come out of his room without her permission.

John's mother then just went for it, but he did not know, so he went to his door, holding it, asking her why don't she just kill him already because he could not take her bulling him anymore.

John's mother then just turned around and threw the knife at him, but before she had thrown it at him, he had already seen it in her hands, so he had shut the door, then all John heard was a big knock on his door.

When John had opened the door back up, to see if she had thrown the knife, all John saw was the knife in his door, not on the floor, so he started thinking he was as quick as all those Power Rangers that he had been hearing about.

John started wanting his brothers to sleep with him at nighttime. Therefore, she could not go over him at night and kill him because she would only come over him to kill him whenever nobody was around.

One night, he had a rough day with his mother because she had told his girlfriend Jessica that he was cheating on her when she had found Jessica's number in his school planner.

John had told his mother to stop holding back and kill him because he has nothing, only his two brothers to live for, but they have a family to help them out in all their tribulations and to take care of them because they love them. "So go ahead and take your anger out on me because I counted how long you and that man were married and my age, and my teacher agreed that it does not match up. Also, because I know your jealous because my grandfather loved me more than you."

John's mother then just looked at him with tears coming down her eyes, telling him, "Yes, you are a mistake" and that she had never loved him or wanted him in her life.

John then started to become fearless during his beatings, he would not even cry no more. He had just started staring right back at her as she would try to beat him and because all he would do was just stare at his mother hard in her eyes, she would be like, "You want to hit me? Hit me! Be a man for once and hit me, Jonathan, so that they will lock you up and send you back to hell."

John began to hate his life even more than before, and began to hate his mother because she continually threatens him with the desire to kill him.

However, no matter what obstacles came, John felt that he would love his brothers, no matter what. Even, if they began to hate him also.

John's mother then wanted to put John into boot camp when she had heard about it, but she never could have done that because he was not having street problems, he was not really socializing with any one at that time because of so many problems at home. However, he still had problems with girls at school. One had hit him because he was acting as if he was too good to talk to one of them as just a friend.

CHAPTER 7

He was in the seventh grade now, and John told himself, "My mother wants me to die. "My mother wants to kill me, but I never did any of the things she keeps blaming me for, and why has nobody told me that he was not my father?" John kept asking himself day to day.

John kept asking himself, "Is she scared, and is she really from Jamaica? In Jamaica, whenever it was said, it was then done, because he had seen a dead body on the floor before, just lying there because of the mouth that one was said to have had in his or her life. However, his Grandfather would just tell him that, that person was just sleeping, and right before each person had gotten killed he would cover up John's eyes, and tell him to close them and not to open up his eyes until he said so.

Feeling that there was no one that could have helped in life, and then looking up, asking his grandfather, "I thought my Father God really cared about me?" In addition, "If he really does, ask him for me, why am I going through all of this abuse and hate down here on earth?"

John had stopped talking to friends and had stopped doing his schoolwork in middle school because he felt like there was no need to. He never really had any schoolwork anyways because his middle school only gave entertainment with fights and wild girls coming in and out of the boys' bathrooms.

H. D. Perry Middle School was not an ordinary middle school because there were so much young teens in there that was supposed to be in high school. Therefore, it was either you fight or get beat up, not even bullied. Teachers were also getting into fights with students, day after day. Surprisingly, at that the time, no one was getting wrote up and given a referral, not even getting arrested or kicked out. Even the school's principal had his day when he had a whole army after him that security could not hold back, so police were called and everyone pepper sprayed.

John was scared to get into fights because he knew his mother would have beaten the lights out of him at that time. Even when one day in class, an argument was going on and John had been slapped by a girl. Everyone just looked at both of them, but all John did was say, "All right and thank you" because he now got someone to get back at on the last day of school, which he had forgotten about on the last day of the school year.

The reason why though was because they were having Alpha against Beta and Gamma, from two different areas of the school right across from one another, fighting one another for the title as the realest side. Many had gotten injured, even teachers, as John watched, but he could not watch the next battle.

When school was finished and the school bells rang, Alpha and Beta and Gamma had to then come together and take on, not only middle schools but also high schools in a royal rumble. That day and that battle were unforgettable for John because how can someone powerbomb and rock bottom someone smaller than them, and then just leave them in pain on the floor to go and get another.

However, it was then ended by the police with their pepper spray. Nevertheless, some had gotten tazered until they had dropped on the floor in pain. Some teens were taken to the hospital because they had gotten stabbed, cut, or something broken on their body. It was found out that there were more than one thousand teens on the field and in school fighting and hurting one another. John had just ended up badly bruised up, with pain in his back and his neck.

Then there was this girl named Latoya, John had met through his middle school years, but not in school, in church. At first they were always fighting, and telling each other that they hated each other. However, there boy George just saw that they could not keep their eyes off each other. Therefore, George was just like "Just say that you'll like each other," one day when he was over her house because he had known her mother also.

John then asked how he knew that. Therefore, George began saying, "Because of the way how both of you will smile after you will fight and give each other attention for no reason at all." John and Latoya ended up thinking about it while looking at each other and then they said yes to each other, but then just walked away from each other. Finds out that they just did not know how to tell each other and did not have it in each other to do it. Therefore, it just never came to mind whenever they were in front of each other.

They then had gotten to know each other better day after day, and then ended up kissing day after day because both fell in love.

Then after a while in their relationship, he felt that Latoya was the only one, other than Alex and George, that he wanted to be with in life because he began feeling better.

John began to feel happy and to love her in his life because he so was hungry for care and love from someone.

He was young, yes, and not having those real emotions yet for another, but he really wanted a real relationship with someone, and that was what he felt he had with Latoya.

Latoya even had another she was talking to when John asked her to be his girl, but she ended up breaking up with him for John. So that made him feel real good. John felt as if he would do anything to keep her in his life because he was desperate to be loved and to love someone.

They were young, but still they spent nights together kissing and hugging each other whenever they could spend nights at George's house.

At that time, John's mother was not caring where and what he was doing because he was nowhere around her.

John had also gotten close with Latoya's mother, and she was even trying to look out for him with food and any other things that she could provide for him.

John was also so surprised that her mother seemed to have trusted them together alone so much.

In their relationship, John was the girl and Latoya was the man because he would be the one to cry, and not her, after fights with each other. She always thought that he was faking it because of the kind of boy that he was. However, she did not know that he was deeply hurting inside.

They then stayed together for their entire middle school years and more even though they were going to different middle schools. However, they were going to the same church and had the same friends that their parents knew about. They never really told no one about their relationship except for Latoya's mother. So that they could have spent as much weekends and nights together.

They used to go to a lot of places together like the movies and shopping together, but it all was really for Latoya. The best time and moments John would say they had was when at first they went to Rapids Water Park together and they slid down the slides together kissing and more. However, that night because of so much contact with each other, John woke up with blue balls, asking to be taken to the hospital because it felt like they had been dismantled.

When John's mother found out about his relationship with Latoya and all the things they were doing and places that they were going together, she had become jealous, telling John, "Do you think that you're going to have a better relationship with Latoya, than me and my husband? Think again," she told John.

John's mother started calling Latoya's mother and telling her that John has AIDS and Latoya might catch it if she continues to kiss him so much. John's mother began telling her that John was cheating on Latoya with another because she caught him one day when she came home early, and John did not know that she had reached home early.

John's mother started telling John that he had start coming straight home from school or else she would call the police and tell them that John was selling drugs on the streets. However, John did not care because he knew he had no money, clothes, or drugs in his system. But Latoya's mother wanted John to start listening to his mother more now because if he wanted a future with her daughter, "First, you have to honor your mother and father so that you could live a longer life."

Then she had said that she was going to try to get John and Latoya in the same high school, "So just work with me," she told John. When they had finished ninth grade, Latoya's mother kept her word, and allowed them to go to the same high school so that Latoya could help John stay out of trouble and get his schoolwork done.

However, when John and Latoya had began tenth grade, John's mother and father started getting into more and bigger husband-and-wife arguments.

They had gotten into many arguments, but this time there were even bigger fights and words because she was over there saying that he was going around cheating on her again, no love and appreciation for each other was going on. From how their relationship was going, honestly, John was not surprised because they were not even spending any time with each other. John and Latoya were doing more and spending more time with each other, and were not even married or lived close by and that was part of the reason why she was so jealous.

John's mother did not even seem like she was interested in her husband any more or him interested in her. John had not even seen them kiss before since he had come to live with them. So yeah, some men like to kiss and some do not, and that goes the same way for the women, too. Still John knew for a fact that when he would grow up it was going to be different because he already knew that he had loved kissing.

They were not even having breakfast or dinner together unless John had cooked and had put both around the table.

There was no "How was your day, sweetheart," not even any "I love you, baby." They were just taking care of John's brothers as John just stayed on the streets with friends and mostly with his girl.

John even kept on seeing that same condom in his so-called father's draw for about a couple of years. John remembered about it all the time because he needed to start a collection at that time because he did not have any money to buy them from a store.

John ended up taking it without him even noticing that it was taken. That is bad—yeah, I know—because things like that John knew nowadays men cherish.

His parents ended up having arguments night after night, day after day. Then John's father just ended up packing up and sleeping at his mother's house for days. He then came back after John called him because John's mother was just taking it all out on him as if it was his fault, and that he knew again something about his father cheating on her and not saying anything to her about it.

She kicked John out again, so he was sleeping at the parks or at one of his friends' house at nighttime. John's mother then found out so she called all of his friends and asked to speak to their parents. Then told them a lot of lies that John was doing things on the street like selling drugs and stealing. Then it was believed that she was the one that had called John's girl and her mother and told them that she had caught John cheating on her again and she had proof. However, John did not know at first because Latoya was not picking up his phone calls to her because she was familiar with all of John's friends numbers.

John called his father and told him that she had kicked him out because one of his friends' mothers had told him to do so, and she had talked to John's so-called father about it all.

John's so-called father ended up coming back and then picking John up first to take him back home. When John's mother saw his so-called father coming into the house with him, she was like "Where have you been and why haven't you been picking up whenever I call you?"

John's so-called father just stayed calm and ignored her, and then just went to go and check up on his brothers to make sure that they were all right. However, still after he walked away and ignored her, she had begun hitting him.

John's mother ended up hitting John's father and slamming him through the wall. John was so surprised that his so-called father took all of that and not even put one hand on her. Therefore, John took her off him so that he could have taken himself from the wall.

After John's so-called father got up, he had told John, "I'll handle it from here," and he held her down.

He was on top of her, looking into her eyes straight and deeply, asking himself questions.

Then he got up after about an hour and left her in the house still all mad and grouchy.

After that day, John's father started coming back but started sleeping on the couch because he did not want to divorce her. However, he then changed his mind and divorced her because of her attitude, so talk toward him. Well, not really, she wanted to divorce him first because she still thought he was cheating on her. However, this time she actually asked the questions to him.

Surprisingly, she ended up blaming it all on John. She was saying that he knew that he was cheating on her and he never told her, John was like "Didn't your man tell that he was not?" She said she did not believe one word that came out of his mouth.

John's mother then wanted John out also. Therefore, she kept kicking him out of the house, and he was sleeping on the streets again day by day, night after night. But since his brothers were there, he was able to get back in the house time after time, and then they would just start arguing out of nowhere for no reason about why was he back in her house.

She kept blaming things on John over and over again, and it just all kept getting to him. She was telling John that she hated him and wanted him to die. John used to cry and just hit walls, screaming out that he could not take it all anymore.

So John began breaking things, and telling her that she better start leaving him alone, before he end up in hell for giving her what she been wanted him to attempt and that was to kill her. She just used to be like, "Yes, that's what I want you to do, and that's to kill me, or he too scared, and if so just hit her."

John's mother then said, "As a matter of fact, I want you to kill me," so then she had gone and got a knife and to gave it to John. But then John was like, "I'd rather kill myself."

John's brothers used to always tell him that they did not want him to kill himself, but he wanted to do it. So badly because he wanted them to have a mother to grow up with and if he killed her, they would not have one.

She never used to treat them the way she treated John because he believed now that his father had raped her.

Day after day, whenever it was just John and her, she would go in the kitchen and get a knife, trying to put it in John's hands. While telling him to stab her, but John was thinking that she just wanted him to put his fingerprints on it, so she could have proof for whenever the police came.

She started to call the police on him every day, every hour trying to get him arrested because she wanted him out. John's mother even busted and scratched up herself just to get him arrested. However, she did it on the wrong day because that same day, before he had went inside, the cops came and told him to stay a certain feet away from her and he did. So when she had called the police on him that day, they found that she was lying and looking like she was about to commit suicide.

Therefore, the police now had a reason to write a report about it all. Then they started sending the child protection agency to search the house for drugs and weapons. They then found none and asked John's brothers questions. They had then told John's mother to watch out because they were going to catch her if she was doing anything wrong in her home with children.

Three days later, John's mother called the police on him eight times in one day, and all they would tell him was to stay away from her because they already knew about the case, and that it was him that they saw a couple nights sleeping on benches at the parks and then running. However, they did not know his name to make a report or what school he had been going to.

At school, John was feeling with his girl Latoya on him, and telling him that she loved him and he would tell her back that he loved her also.

Then that same day that John felt that he had finally made love to his love, his mother had finally got him arrested when he had just flipped in the house and went crazy because his mother kept on sounding as if she was going to make him lose Latoya. John broke the pictures on the wall and really everything that was anywhere around him at that time of that argument between him and his mother.

John's mother then tried to press eight different charges against him, however only one went through and that was for breaking walls in the house and pictures, so destruction of property. Nevertheless, she began telling the judge I had been hitting her, threatening her, stealing money, and was doing drugs on the street. John already was already feeling stressed so he just told the judge straight up, "Yes," and that she could believe everything that his mother was telling them because he wants twenty-five years in prison or even life because he rather that before he ends up doing something wrong and then end up in hell.

"Put me on the—electric chair because I want to die!" John then screamed out and told them. The judge, officers, and every other person in the courtroom were just looking at him in silence as if he was crazy.

The judge then said, "You need some serious help, boy!" In addition, they would have to start family therapy and he would have anger management with his own psychiatrist, therapist, and on medication.

So now on the weekends, John had anger-management classes, and he had to keep on going to therapy because his probation officer was feeling sorry for him and decided that he really needed it in his life because of how much rage he was showing, and how much it seemed like he had hiding inside of him.

They would have locked him up if he had not been attending all his classes, not in juvenile detention center but in a mental home, for some personal talk.

John's therapist was saying that he seemed like he was feeling down, upset, and unloved in this world, which was true because his girl was not as close with him no more.

John told her that he has nobody here in America other than his brothers and his girlfriend, that he feels he was about to lose because of lies.

So his therapist wanted him to make some plans to help him get his life and mind back in order, and the main thing that she knows that had him down was his relationship with his mother.

The therapist was like, "Go to your mother and ask her if she loves you, and when you hear the answer, come back and tell me how you feel," so John decided to do it the next morning.

Ever since that day after they went to court—some caseworkers had a talk with his mother about child neglect. Therefore, she would walk around him now and not through him.

The next morning, John had to beg his mother to sit down with him because he had something that he wanted to ask her and because he had never asked her this question before. John then said, "I've gone through a hard life with you, and I feel very depressed, and weak deep inside. I've always felt unloved and unwanted in my life since I had gotten here from Jamaica, and I don't really understand why you treat me this way. Therefore, I am just going ask you this question because you have never told me this before since I have come from Jamaica. Well, since I was younger." Therefore, John asked her, "Do you love me, Mother?"

She then looked into John's eyes and said, "No, Jonathan. I never did because I hate you. I never wanted you in my life, and I wish you would've just died instead of coming into my life, causing nothing but drama and pain for me."

"How can you put everything that you go through in your life on me?" John asked her.

"Because I can, and if you have a problem, there's nothing that you can do about it." John's mother then told him.

Then John's mother got up, picked up her stuff, and left the house with him in there by himself. John's brothers were at their grandma's house, so he sat down home alone with his head down. John sat down around the table for quite some time, quiet and crying. John's fists began balling up and his tears began to drop down his eyes.

John's heart began beating hard as he began to pressure his mind, his mind then felt like it was about to explode, and he then began getting very dizzy.

"—this world, everything, everyone, and—my life, and where is my—father when I—truly need him, does not he promise to always be around for his—children. My brothers do not—really need me, because they have a—father and a—family around them that—loves and—care for them.—You father and your words—saying that you are here at my—side. Where the—are you then. I am tired of the—ones telling me that they—love me, and they really do not."

John then began to let out all of the anger and the temptations that he was waiting to let go. However, not on someone, he began to let it all out by breaking things and hitting himself and slamming his head against walls.

John then cursed his Father for not being there for him, and telling to strike him down right now. So John went outside and looked up with fright but wanting and said, "Here I'm—ready. Kill me," because he had once heard that if one ever does that they would have gotten stricken down right then and there.

John then started laughing, saying, "I thought you were really up there, but now you have proven to me that you are not. I still believe in spirits though, but I do not know if I can ever believe in you again."

John then went back inside laughing and at the same time crying hard while looking at "him" in the mirror. John started wondering if he was "really, really" meant to be here on earth because his mother was raped and not loved by that man who was his father.

Looking deeply at him, John then said, "—my life," and then started walking with his head down toward the kitchen because he did not want to look at another picture of his brothers.

John then woke up watching TV. When his mind and memory came back, he asked himself how he reached here because the last thing he remembered was coming from outside. "Did the Lord struck me down?" he asked himself because he did remembered that he was saying wrong things to his Father.

John's body was in pain, especially his head, it felt like it was swollen. His fist, arms, and chest were bleeding and all scratched up. He had then looked around and saw that the cereal box, which he had taken out before he had talked to his mother, was still out.

John then looked outside, it was dark, and he still had on those same boxers and shirt from when he had awakened. John then went inside and looked at himself in the mirror. His eyes were red, and his lip was busted; his tongue had been bitten really hard. However, it had stopped bleeding. He did not know what had happened to him at all.

John kept questioning himself and looking around his mother's home. John then saw a lot of things broken, he was not feeling like he had strength in him so went to go lie down, he then fell asleep with it all on his mind.

John woke up for school the next day, after another heartbroken day had occurred, with a huge headache, but he did not want to stay home so he went to school.

John made sure he kissed his girl hello first, and then went straight to class and put his head face down on the desk before class had even started.

He slept through that whole period but then while coming out from class and going toward another, his head started feeling like there was something pounding in there, and he just began spinning in his mind.

Getting dizzier with things running through his mind, John could not believe it, everything around him were moving, and he was seeing double then saying, "I am about to die," he just had a blackout, right then and there in the school's hallway.

John had then waken back up two days later in the hospital and they told him that he had a total of sixteen seizures in the hospital since he was there and now on the third day, he has not had any yet. The doctor had told John that he was lucky to be still alive because that was really a near death experience for a young teen like me in a situation like that, at only fourteen years old.

In the hospital, with all the nurses watching over him closely, John had no one there by his side, "—everyone else then," John then said. As a result of it, he then had some more seizures, so the doctors decided to increase the dosage of medication that they were giving to him.

When they had increased medication dosage for John as if he was an adult, some of the dizziness had gone away, but then John could not stay awake. Therefore, they had to decrease it a little, but he then ended up having more seizures, so the doctors said, "We are just going to have to keep you on a high dosage of medication because you can die anytime if you keep on having all those seizures like that."

They then took John to get his head examined and it seemed as if something busted in his head and he had either a tumor of some sort growing in his brain, so they called a neurologist to examine John's brain problems.

"Jonathan, we already know that you're stressed and that is one of the problems, but also you have something growing in your brain. Therefore, you need to stop stressing out yourself, we are going to have to bring someone up here to watch because every time you have a seizure you always want to fight someone," the doctor said.

"So tell me, Jonathan, what has been bothering you so much, what has been stressing you out so much? And don't tell me you do not have a guardian watching over you and helping you in life. Because no one has even come yet since you have been in the hospital, so can I have your mother's or father's number?" "I don't have one," John then said, and all the doctor did was look at him and said OK.

They then took all the IVs out of John because he kept on complaining about it, and they were not trying to make John mad. So now, John could have walked around feeling free until they had gotten the results that the doctors were waiting on.

The next day, they had said that John had, had another seizure and had wanted to kill himself during it, but John had no memory of it all. Therefore, the doctors began not wanting John out of their sight and the hospital anytime soon.

John began trying to leave as soon as he could because he felt there could never be anyone there for him like Latoya, he did not want to lose her, so he felt the best thing he could have done to keep her was to get out of the hospital to go and see her.

His mother still did not go to the hospital yet, so they told him that he could not be released until some papers were signed for approval of some things that he needed.

He was having unbelievable images in his head, back to back, of himself getting killed, watching others look over him as he lay in a casket, with everyone smiling and laughing, and having a wonderful time still, even though he was lying down dead in front of them.

John did not cry though because at least he can see himself in the coffin before he get there, and how others would be looking at him, if he even have a funeral.

They had finally let him out of the hospital when they had got in contact with his mother. So now, John went back into his mother's home after so many days in the hospital. "I wished you would have died while you were in the hospital" was all his mother had to say to him. John then walked to his room and cried because that was not even a small situation that had just occurred, and those were words that he would expect from an enemy. Those were the words that his friend's father said to a man, a day before he died, in Jamaica. Therefore, "If she really wants it, she is going to get it," John told himself.

That night, John's brothers were there, trying to find out what was wrong with John because he had ended up on the floor. With his mother over him asking him if he was finish yet because he began to have more seizures. However, it was not until he got mad, got up, and went outside that he ended up right back in the hospital because of all the thoughts that he kept in his mind about his mother.

Doctors did not know what to do with him except put him on some strong medication that would just put him straight to sleep night and day for relaxation. The doctors then ran a whole bunch of tests again before he was able to go back home.

The doctors wanted to know what was causing him to have such a brain disorder at such a young age, if it really was one. Therefore, his mother kept telling them that he was on drugs, so they tested him for drugs before he left and found none in his system.

After looking over his background and his present situation, doctors then found out that he was in therapy because he had a lot held in him, so he was in a deep depression they figured out, with a lot of anger wanting to come out but was being held in.

One doctor had then told John that he could die anytime, because he was holding in too much and not even putting interest in staying alive. Therefore, it was really up to him, to stay strong, to let out his anger so that he could live a longer life.

The doctors then told his mother that he would be needing surgery or else he might have an 80 percent chance of dying, but she kept telling them no because he was the one that was causing it all on himself, and then for what was growing in his head he would just have to live with it there.

John then went back to his mother about it and asked her why they cannot do the surgery. "Because I want you to die," she then told him.

He had to go back to school now, but because of too much unexcused absences, John ended up going back with everyone just watching, not knowing when he was going to drop. However, what began to have fewer eyes on him was when he wanted to fight everyone saying because he hated everyone. Therefore, he was given space day until day in school.

His tenth grade school year ended with much more about to end his life.

John had then went to see his therapist because he had found out that he had a warrant out for his arrest. Therefore, he went and told them all that had happened to him because they wanted to know why he had not made any phone calls to tell them that he could not come.

After it was all explained to his therapist and psychiatrist, they told John that right now, he needs to file child-neglect charges, with no investigation needed because of his doctors and school and that they will handle the warrant that was out for him. In addition with it all now, "John, to what you had asked us one time, no, we do not see you living a long life."

When John's mother had found out about what was about to happen, she had called one of her friends to talk to John for her. So that he would not continue with what his psychiatrist and therapist had started for him because they had told her that John's brothers had to go and live with their father until it all was finished and John began living with Lori.

Lori had then explained to John what had happened to his mother and why she treated and thought of him as an enemy. Lori had then explained to him that his mother had went on a date with his father one night, and his mother did not want to have sex with him. However, he really wanted to, he decided to rape her, but she never pressed any charges on him because of the kind of person he was, so she was scared, too. "So now, whenever she sees you, she sees him and all that he had done to her that night. So understand why she treats you like that, and says the things she does and she felt that by hitting you, she is finally fighting back now."

"So I was a mistake then right, Lori?" "Yes, you can say that. However, you are not a mistaken child toward your Father God," Lori then told John.

Thinking in his head now about it all, John began having more understanding, but then more not wanting to live.

"Therefore, it seems like what she went through with my birth father explains the maltreatment in my life, and she was just expressing what she wanted to express out on my birth father, out on me. I was a mistaken birth that had taken place right, Lord, when my mother had come to America, my father touched someone that he was not supposed to touch, right. Therefore, whenever she saw or thought of me, I guess he came to mind, and what had taken place that night, OK?" John then said.

Thinking about his brothers, he was wondering if they were not his real brothers, then. Not caring, he told himself that, he loved his brothers because that was what they will always be to him, they were the only ones that he feels will always think of him, and love him until the end of time.

"I never would want my brothers to go through what I have been through in my life here on earth," John then told himself. Even though he was beating them up all the time and doing things to them to get them mad and embarrassed, he still and will always love them.

Thinking of his brothers, he now thought back when they used to play together, and when they were home alone, all the things that used to happen like if one was not crying, the other was laughing at the other getting beat up. Then when both ended up laughing at him one day when they threw ice water under his sheets, and then ran for their lives, locking themselves in their mama's room until she came home, and they even slept with her that night for safety, under her arms.

Therefore, no matter what, he told himself he would not want them to live a messed up life like how he have lived. So since they enjoy being with their mother so much, he will not make those complaints and mess up their lives with their mother unless their mother start treating them the same way she was treating him.

He then started telling all of his old teachers and friends' mothers that through all of his life problems that he had went through, he was never innocent. With all that he was going through because he used to break things, screaming back at her, and telling her that he wished he were never her son. Cursing back at her and telling her that she was going to go to hell with him for all of this.

Telling her what his father did to her was not his fault and that it was her choice to go on a date with him, not his.

John then found out last that the real reason why her friend came out of nowhere and told him all of that. They were all being told that he was going to die soon and if he was going to die, what was the sense of locking her up because he would no longer be around.

John's mind about his life calmed down when he was living with Lori, Monica, Tiffany, and Tim for a while. John was not being stressed, screamed at, or anything else, and so he began to get better in life with all those thought out of his head.

Charges were dropped and his brothers returned back home to his mother, but his psychiatrist and therapist was not happy with that, so they requested that it remained open because of how much times now his mother was supposed to be arrested and given time since John was in elementary school.

The one thing that John had to get back now was his relationship with Latoya, the same way that it used to be. So to accomplish that, he had to start hanging out with his girl again, and proving to her that he still loved her through it all, even though she was never there for him, through it all.

Entertaining Tim day after day because in a way they were celebrating that he had finally gotten better now, and could start getting some loving from his girl again.

One night, John had Tim's stomach hurting and eyes red on the floor, while John was there lying on the bed mad because Tim used to laugh at John so much for so much he would start back doing, that was bad. It was one day after school, John went straight to Latoya house, and they were saying, "Let's try something new," while they had their so-called lovemaking thing going on, but differently that day.

When John had made it back to Tim's house, before he entered the house, he was wondering why he could not get this smell from out of his nose. It was a new scent for him, so John went in making up his face. Tim looked at John while he was lying on the bed with his face made and he had just come out the bathroom washing his face and brushing his teeth, "What's wrong?" so John was like, "I can't get this smell out my nose."

Tim knew John was young and inexperienced with a couple of things; he and his girl just kept on kissing and making out the same way, day after day. Therefore, the woman he had when he was young and she was in her midthirties did not do much for him.

Tim was then like, "Did you just come from your girl's house?" So John said, "Yeah." Therefore, Tim said, "Why you didn't tell her to take care of the smell in your nose for you?"

John then said, "Because she caused it, fool! I did not want to make her feel bad." "Mr. Bad Boy, do not tell me you did it already." John felt he had to do something to make her happy, so he did not care. "I thought you were going to wait until you were married, John" Tim asked him. "I want her," John told Tim. Then Tim just dropped on the floor while he was eating, right in front of Jonathan, laughing at him, choking on his food. That night, Tim just kept laughing and looking at John as he brushed and washed out his mouth with Listerine all night, including scrubbing his lips.

The next day, John was on the couch reading poems that he had written, while thinking about his love. Tim just laughs at him, saying that he could tell he was lying, asking John how much time he had to go to rehearsal for just one line and how long did it take him to write one word.

While trying to give all of his love to Latoya day after day, he was also wondering how his brothers were doing. Therefore, he made Tim call and ask for them and they had told John that they were doing all right. However, when their mother heard them talking to John, she took the phone away from them and told John to never call her phone again.

John was like, "I told them that I was not going to press any charges, so why you still mad me for?" Because they were still coming to her house questioning her children about how she was treating them.

That same night, John stayed home by himself because he got mad at his mother, she could have been locked up if it was not for him.

Latoya had then called John at about 9:00 p.m., and told John, "I do not want to, but then again I'm sorry but I'm just going to have to end the relationship between us, so bye," not allowing John to say a word to her.

John had still held the phone to his head because he now had it in his mind now that he was now talking to his Father in heaven. "So now one of the last ones I loved in my life is now gone while you was making my life better, Father, OK, and I was told to give thanks to my Father every day now in my life, and everything he does for me. THANK YOU! In addition, I LOVE YOU!"

John then leaned up against the wall and then dropped on the floor crying.

Crying on the floor that night, John built up anger inside himself. Then started asking himself, why she ended it? No one was home with him. Therefore, he just got and went to his bed with a lot going through his mind.

"I know my time and days are going down, just like the ones that I have and love in my life. However, no matter what, my brothers will always be my brothers no matter what because I found out that we are still blood brothers, we have the same mother," John told himself.

Wanting to be on his own, John packed up and left, dropping off some clothes at his mother's house, telling his brothers to hold on to them for him and also at other friends' houses. Walking the streets telling himself that no one could help him through all the things he had to face day by day.

Still, talking to his therapist because he had to and they had made him feel comfortable with them. Therefore, during summer he had to go to them at least three times a week, but did not tell them where he was living now. John started to cry each time he talked to them about his life. Therefore, they were like, things happen for a reason in life and for him to just believe, and have faith that our Lord and Savior Jesus Christ will take him through all, and they knew that John had it in himself again to just commit suicide, so they mentioned walking through heaven naturally, not when he wanted to.

In addition, they had already predicted a short life for John.

Therefore, so that John would not sit down thinking about the past, they gave John a compact disk player to listen to music of his choice. One of his big hits at that time was "Hell for a Hustler" because of the true feeling he felt from it. Therefore, he wanted Tupac Shakur compact disk, so they went and got one for him. They had then asked John, "I thought you loved love songs." "Yeah," he told them, "but it matters how I am feeling and wanting. Anyways since I came to America and listening to all, I feel he is true just like how my uncles and grandfather used to describe Bob Marley to me." "Well, this is going to be the last rap compact disk, with all these batteries, we are going to buy you since you said he is your favorite."

However, in return they wanted John to allow them to do some kind of hypnosis, so he said all right, as long as it do not mess his mind and life up. They had first started by bringing out some kind of book, with another language on it so he could not understand the words.

"Lie down calm and relax," the therapist and psychiatrist then told John.

"Breathe in and then breathe out, stay calm and relax your mind, and now start repeating after me," the therapist then told John.

After some time, John listened to himself answering every question they were asking him about his life, past, and future. The things that he held in so dearly, were what they were going for in his mind.

When they were finished, John was like, "Don't you ever do something like that to me again," because as he had let them in his mind, he could not take them out.

That was one day John will never "ever forget" in his life.

John started walking with it all in his ear day and night, Tupac was describing the way he felt and the things he felt he also had to do to survive. Sleeping on the streets again day by day and then showering at his mother's house or friends, John wanted it all that way and for it to stay the same. John began to go back and forth to Miami because he had made so many friends, and their parents that were living a rough life also. He was interested to see homeless people on the streets night and day because he used to pass by them in a car all the time. Wondering how they used to feel, he saw that they were not as happy as he was on the streets because they had no one to help them, so he gave one the ten dollars his friend's mother gave him to get where he need to be day after day.

John was only sixteen at this time, with so many people trying to help him, even though he kept telling them that he does not need anyone.

With John talking to many ministers, his friends' mothers were all like, "We do not want you here bringing trouble on yourself," because all John would want to do was to fight another older man and then get beat up repeatedly. However, John would never run whenever he was about to be jumped, only taking it hoping that he would die.

Therefore, friends did not become enemies, enemies became friends, giving him love and support, and telling him, he was one crazy young man, and he needed to do better and get smarter. If some never knew about him, and all the parents he had known, John would have been killed, and no one would have known because everyone knew that he traveled a lot, and never stayed in one spot.

However, he brought it all on himself because of wanting someone to fight and then be jumped up, every day in the end. Standing still with a gun in his face, wanting it and asking for it, he was considered a real young man with a real Jamaican background and because of the fact that he was so crazy in life, he was not caring if he lived or died.

There were more Haitian background people than Jamaicans out there, including Spanish, but looking at them all and then thinking back, John then developed that belief that we are all still one, no matter what, color does not mean a thing, it was all about our minds and how we have grown feeling in this world.

The next week came and so he went back up north to go and see his therapist and psychiatrist. When he had then went back, they had told him that before he leaves, they have something to tell him. The therapist started talking to him, asking him how has he been doing and feeling, and how has the music been making him feel. "The same really," he told her but with knowledge and understanding of why he said and did the things he said he would do to any other except his mother, whom he had arguments with also.

The therapist then listened to it and said that he must have some deep aggression inside him.

"That one rap song sounds the same way I feel, I feel it while I used to listen to it. While it yes, built more rage in me. However, it ended with 'Lord, help me change my ways.'" That was the only part his therapist would play repeatedly, and then she would just start preaching to John.

Therapist was like, "Even though you're mad at your Father God right now for all that you're going through, still you want to make it to heaven, right?" and she was like, "Your brothers are alive right?" John said yes, "So why aren't you happy?" she asked him. Because I want someone to love," John then told her.

"You are still alive, right?" In addition, John was like, "In a way I don't care, but then again, yes."

"Committing suicide will send you straight to hell, if that's in your mind. Moreover, you wont leave your brothers alone because what if the same things that you are going through start happening to them in the future? Where would you be?" So John then said, "All right, I understand so now, no more preaching, and tell me before I go what you wanted me to know."

"Oh, the police said you have another warrant out for your arrest, but I will not say that I saw you, OK? Just make the right choices, all right, and I already knew that you were living, walking around the streets," the therapist then said.

John then went back down to South Miami by taking the bus and told his friend's mother, and all she said was get into the car, and took John right back home to his mother, and gave him her cell phone number.

When John's mother had seen John outside being dropped off, she immediately called the police. But John's friend's mother had already left when they had reached the house and they did not take John, they just reported that he was found and was now back in his mother's home. They then gave Jonathan the woman's card that was working for the Child Neglect Department and told him to make sure that he is home tomorrow because she is going to come and speak with him and his mother.

The next day, the woman came and she did not have a nice attitude because she said her words to John's mother as if she was threatening her, telling her one more call, and she is gone. Then she took John outside and told John to stop being so damn scared to talk because look at how big John had gotten now, he had started working out and lifting weights when he was on the streets. So instead of John getting skinny while he was living on the street, John had gotten bigger from 225 pounds while he was in the hospital, to now 255 pounds.

They had then told John's mother to put him into school so that he could start back up school again. Therefore, John started going to his third high school, and it was that school's first year because it had just been finished being constructed on.

Somehow, living in a quiet neighborhood with a lot of the children's parents making big money, that school had become a bad school with a lot of fights going on because of how people talked to one another while they were showing off their jewelry, clothes, money, and cars that their parents had bought them. Therefore, fights were happening because of not only jealousy but also provoked by another.

There were thugs and gangster that were all hyped up by all the rap and hip-hop music being made, played, and loved by all. Therefore, everyone wanted to be a 305 representative by saying, "I am from the hood, so do not look or mess with me or else you are going to get beat up because I am from the ghetto."

Some students were tough but then taken out for a better and brighter future but had still decided to continue being a thug in life. However, whenever they were "locked up" in a cell and could not get out without the judge saying so, that was when many would change in their selves in life and say, "This street life and fighting is not right in my life."

Drug busts by security guards and administrators were going on in there continuously because that school was a great school to sell drugs in. Ninety percent of the students in there had money to get the drugs that they wanted to smoke, inject, swallow, and sniff.

John was not a known student in there at first because he had never gone out to any schools in that certain area before. Therefore, he never talked to anyone in the beginning of the school year of 2003-2004. Seeing many beautiful young girls, John began wanting to stay but needed money because he had no clothing compared to all the other students.

Borrowing clothing from other friends from time to time who did not go to that same school that he had started attending, John started feeling as if he was finally able to walk up to one of them school girls and ask them either for a number or some of their time.

Up against the wall at lunchtime and quiet in all his classes, John had never had to because they all would come to him but only wanting to speak with him privately with not another knowing as if they were ashamed to be seen with him.

They just never wanted the crowd to know their business and then get called a hoe. Therefore, they only went up to certain ones that they felt could keep their mouths shut and would not tell the world for fame.

After a day with a new friend named Cassandra whom John was getting to know day after day after school, John's mother had seen her car pulling out of the drive way. However, when she had gone inside of the house, she had never said anything to John about it. Looking at John face to face, she said, "I am going to get you back for that."

"For what, what did I do to you now?" John had then asked her.

John's mother had just then went inside of her room and had taken a shower sounding like she was crying.

Not knowing it, John's mother had called the police on him.

Sitting down watching television in the living room, John saw his mother crying, with scratches and marks on her face and body, while she was about to walk out the front door.

"She's crazy," John then laughed and said.

Police then came inside of the house and turned off the television, telling John to stay seated.

"Why did you beat up your mother, little boy, and then try to rape her?"

"You were having problems finding a girlfriend?" the police asked John.

"What are you talking about?" John then asked them, "And if you are talking about all those marks that I had just seen on her body when she had came out her room, she did that all by herself; and if you want to believe her go ahead because you will be the fools for believing her."

"Why would your mother lie about something about that then, you tell me?" the police then asked John.

"She hates me. Look it up in your computer system about how many problems me and my mother already had in the past," John then replied to the officers.

"I was sitting down right here on the couch, and I am guessing that she must have seen the girl that I had here in her house, leaving her house just now. Because she told me that she was going to get me back for something when she came in the house."

"You better not be lying to us," the police then said to John.

"Anyways, look how big my hands and arms are, if I would have grabbed her, and abused, and then tried to rape her, you would have seen her swollen, fools! So do not believe her lies but if you want to arrest me, you can go ahead."

"No! We are not," the police then said. "Because what you are saying is true. Therefore, we are going to go and talk to her about this."

When the police had then finally left, John's mother had run inside crying, saying, "Why can't I get you out?" She then ran inside of the kitchen and went after John with a knife. John had then moved out the way and had seen the knife go into the couch so he was in his mind saying, "She is not playing with me this time."

Going after John with the intent to kill him, she just kept telling him to die. So John held her down on the couch and told her that if she expect to be able to kill him, ask first and probably he might allow her. Looking into her first having a serious face but then a big smile on her face laughing, John's mother just began telling John to get off her.

Smiling also, John told her that she has no chance of fighting and killing him face to face, he had to be sleeping for her to have a better opportunity to take his life.

"I was not trying to kill you," John's mother then told him. "I was trying to see if you knew how to defend yourself just in case someone ever tries to kill you."

"Sure, you were not!" John then told his mother. "You were just trying to put new decorations in like holes in your sofa and also in me but I never wanted any, so I had to wrestle with you and then hold you down to tell you, no!"

"What do you want for dinner?" John's mother then asked John. She wants a big dinner tonight with John at her side, who is her son that she loves so dearly, ever since he had been born.

John had then looked at her with tears in his eyes coming down because he knew that she was lying to save herself from being locked up and told her that she does not have to lie and tell him that she loves him.

Punching the wall, John then said, "I wish that I had never had you in my life," Each time he had thought that he was loved and was really not after every case was dropped.

"Do you know how it feels inside of me?" John then asked his mother.

"No! Because I do not truthfully care," John's mother then said to him.

"Thank you," John then said to his mother.

"For what?" she then asked John.

"For telling the truth, and I wished you have told my grandmother and grandfather that same thing before they had let me go," John then told her as he walked out the front door.

CHAPTER 8

John started talking back to friends around where his mother had just recently moved in and at the same time looking for another to come in and then not back out. Hearing his first favorite love song again on the radio since he had first came to America, and that was Mary J. Blige singing "Real Love." Tim had always laughed at him whenever they were going to bed because as Tim used to listen to the Hot Boys and feeling hyped not being able to sleep, John just used to listen to "Real Love" and with his eyes closed feeling relaxed, falling asleep.

John started talking to a girl after a couple of days, after he had started back going to school, and her name was Cindy, but she was not for him because he was already unhappy and he did not want to have any more arguments with another. Moreover, that was all they were doing because she wanted it all her way. John had continued talking to her because after every break up, she would just call, asking John to forgive her. Therefore, he just kept it going, trying to work it all out with her since he would be seeing her crying.

After school, John would go and take the bus up to Cindy's house to go and spend time with her because he felt he had one to hold every day, and he was beginning to like her. She played on her school's band so she was in shape at that time, and because John was big at that time, he wanted a thick one not a small one.

John had gotten to know Cindy's mother and two younger brothers and was just introduced to her older sister who did not really live there with them, so he seldom saw her. Cindy's mother thought of John as a thug just trying to have sex with girls, but after some talks with John, she had then realized that he was looking for love because he felt some way.

At the new school that John was going, he had begun befriending a couple of them in there, but mostly the ones that he would be with at the bus stop in the mornings. Therefore, he started to hang out with some of them, after school on the days that Cindy had practice or a game to play at.

One day, John and two friends that he had made, named Mario and Kevin were hanging out, they were bored so Mario was like, "Crazy John, come on, I'm going to introduce you to this new girl that had just moved into our neighborhood, it seems like, nobody knew about her around here. Until she had introduced herself to someone, and when you go over, keep your mind calm so that you will not have any seizures, I had heard you had one in school the other day."

In addition, "You never know, she might like you, she doesn't really have a man right now because the relationship she is in right now with someone that had said he knew John from tenth grade said it is nothing going on really between them, just talk."

When they had gotten there, Mario was like, "The first one to get a kiss is a real pimp all right, but I do not see any competition so I already know that I am the pimp."

However, John was like "you're all fools, go ahead, and compete" because he already had a girl. When she had opened up, Mario gave her a hug hello, saying, "This is my homeboy Crazy John and John this is my home girl Tamika."

Tamika looked like a happy girl because she was there smiling with every word that was coming out of her mouth. When they went inside, John already knew that she liked Mario because of the way she would just be giving him all her attention. So John just went out her back patio door, she saw John walk out but he did not even know that she was paying attention to him. Outside thinking about a couple of things especially how nice her home was looking with a lake behind of it, that he felt like jumping in. Outside thinking nobody noticed, Tamika then came out to ask John if he was all right and why he does not want be inside with them.

Tamika then asked John if he had wanted someone to talk to, looking up at him with a smile on her face. John told himself, "You never know she might be that special one that you had been asking God to bring in your life." Therefore, it would be stupid of him to just, let a girl like her pass. However, at the same time with everything he was seeing her interested in; he was feeling that he would not be able to become anything in her life.

John was then like that he would like to be her friend, but she asked first because it seemed like he was so scared to ask her.

They then started talking to each other day after day whenever her father was not there because he was protective of his household.

At the same time of talking and getting to know Tamika, John was still dating Cindy but not going to her house as much no more because he became more interested in Tamika.

Tamika used to talk to John as if she was John's full time therapist and psychiatrist like the ones he had started seeing once a month. However, more loving and seemed to have really gotten into John in a short period because John started liking her even though they were only best friends.

Tamika then introduced John to her mother, cousin, and younger sister who were all loving just like her. However, he was sure that they all had it, grown in them by Tamika's mother.

However, during nights in the dark alone by himself, under the covers or pillow over his head, it was not Tamika's mother that had John crying with a smile on his face and giving God thanks for all the happiness now in his life. It was Tamika, the one that he thought he would have never became friends with and the one that he thought would not have given him any attention. Tamika had John listening to "Angel from Above" by K-C and Jojo and "I Believe in You and Me" by Whitney Houston because he felt that she was the one that God had sent down to hold him and be with him for the rest of his life, with happiness and everlasting love.

John would shake with a funny feeling inside of him every time when he would be walking up to Tamika to greet her with a hug and a kiss, saying hello. In addition, whenever he would want to hug her with a kiss saying good-bye.

However, Tamika had not realized that at first. She had just believed that John did not have a loving heart with feelings deep inside of him growing for her every time John would be conversing with Tamika, looking into her eyes.

Many times looking into her eyes wanting to cry. John said, "I love you," but only when he would look at her pictures on her family's house wall.

Therefore, they would just shake each other's hands because in a way she was afraid that John would one day hit her. John wrestled with her one day saying, "I do not want my sister getting beat up so I am going to train." However, he did not know that Tamika had taken it another way.

Cindy and John had ended up breaking up because she wanted to know why John was getting so happy all of a sudden and she was hardly around him, she was so busy. Therefore, there must be another, she then began starting to think so she kept asking John from time to time, if there was another, and John would always tell her that he loves the way his best friend always be making him feel.

However, they always ended up getting back together, but then John was thinking that their relationship definitely has to end because even though he liked every time they held each other, still he was hoping that his friend would become interested in him someday in their lives together as friends.

However, John one day went to a party with some of his homeboys Marcus, Tim, and Mark. John was about two years older than they were, but he still went to a party with them because he was not eighteen yet. John had seen this beautiful girl and her name was Ciara, they had told him, and that she was the same age as them.

Therefore, John was like "Let me see if she can find some time for a poor brother like me." She was beautiful girl, and because he did not want to be turned down in front of everyone, he just asked her to go outside with him. She also had interest in John when she had seen him. They had talked that night and it then just kept on going.

John started to get to know Ciara well. She was a sixteen-year-old girl with a deep desire for success. She was Jamaican, and she just had such a great personality, caring and wanting to talk and be with him, no matter what. He even ended up having seizures in front of her, and all she would do was just lie there beside him and cry until he came back to his right mind.

When John would wake up from a seizure, he would ask her what was wrong, and why she was she crying. She would then just tell him that she would never leave him, and that she would always be there for him because she cares and dreams of a future with him.

John's relationship with her was nice, sweet, and real because she was an intelligent girl, an honor student in school. However, when John had found out that she was his homeboy Anthony's ex-love, he had begun to rethink about their relationship. After he had went at John with a bat, telling him that he could not talk to her no more, but before he could have reached anywhere near John, his homeboy held him back.

"If he would have come up to me right, I would have probably rethink my relationship with you," John told Ciara. "But he ended up making me wanting to be with you more because it seems like one always fight for true happiness I receive."

John and Latoya were still getting closer with one another at that time, even though they both had another in their young lives. Although, John was spending most of his time with Ciara, John was right there thinking and hoping to be with that one he loved right now in his life. He had her picture in his wallet and mind, picturing her in front of him, asking her to let him be the one to love her more than anyone in her lifetime.

However, because of how much time they spent together, Ciara had felt that John had taken her off track in school, but never wanted to tell him. However, John noticed it because of her attitude toward wanting John to come in by a certain time, and out by a certain time. So that she could have time to finish her schoolwork on time.

John had then told her that the best thing do was to end it because of her dreams. She had told him about where and how she would love to be in life with a man with a good job, making money loving her, and caring for her.

"Dreams like that with me in your life will never be seen." John then told her because he was not having faith in himself that he could make it through life.

John regretted it but she had always wanted him happy and safe, so now he thought, now he would do the same for her.

John's mother had then kicked him out that night because she was saying that John thinks he could just walk in and out of her house whenever he wanted and then eat her food without asking her.

John then began living with different friends again, so he kept meeting different girls. But not everyone liked John in the same way that John liked them, especially his best friend Latoya because she only thought of him as a brother, and she was that one that John mostly had his mind on.

John had met back up with this one girl named Latisha. Even though he did not even have her for more than a month, they still had a close relationship because they were friends at first. It all started one night, while he was walking with her because she loved to exercise. While they were talking, she had mentioned that she loved the attitude that John was developing, so she would love a boyfriend like John in her life because of how independent he was becoming at such a young age.

Therefore, John was like, "So you love me then." She had then said she did not know, so John was like, "Let's see if you'll talk to an ugly brother like myself." She used to always have one of those so-called pretty boys as her boyfriend—neat, clean, brush cut, waves, jewelry, and money.

So John kissed her and looked her in the eyes. She then said, "It's my turn now to see if you really like me," so she just french-kissed John for a good minute and said, "I'm surprised you know how to kiss so slow and romantic," so John was like, "There's much more that she does not know about him."

They then started to go out and doing almost everything together, she used to pay for everything because John had no money, and his homeboys that were taking care of him said that John wasn't going to be spending their money on some girl that John didn't even really bring home to meet them.

John had never introduced them because he was afraid that she would rather have one their attention than his if they ever met her because they loved to talk.

After a couple of days of spending time with her, John really thought their relationship was real because they once had a strong friendship. He was very nice and gentle with her, but it ended up ending because he kept comparing Latisha with Tamika.

John was wishing for a life with another before he started talking to Latisha because she had never got mad before in front of him only happier every time he was there, so John told Latisha.

Latisha was happy that John was truthful with her and just gave him a kiss and said, "Friends forever and good luck with that one that you feel you truly dream to be with." Latisha had then told John to write to her and tell her how he knew that she was not that one for him. She did not want to hear it face to face, but John still told her because he never knew.

"Mainly because when I was in deep pain and depression, and whenever I felt like I'm going back into darkness, Tamika was more of my light and happiness, whenever I had thought of her and she was not even my girl, so imagine if she becomes," John told her.

John kept moving around so much because he had gotten to know more people. From north to south, then from west to east, it was as if he had nothing else to do with his life but walk the streets and sleep in different beds and places at night.

However, it all helped him out in mind so much because he felt so free, and so stress-free. Nevertheless, the police had then caught him after a fight with someone on the street, so the police had then brought him back to his mother's house because he was walking with clothes in his bag. They had then questioned his mother why he was on the street with his clothes in his bag, and all she was telling them was that John had ran away, when they asked John he did not even answer because he already knew if he made one more complaint, John's mother was going to be charged with child neglect, for now and the past.

John had then started having seizures repeatedly because all his mother would do was just act as if she was despising him, so that then made him feel a certain way. John was then brought back in the hospital because he had a seizure in school on his first day back.

While John was in the hospital and about to finally get released, John's mother had lied and told the doctor that he was going mental because she had seen him doing things to himself at night and taking drugs.

Therefore, the doctor had believed her, and they had then put John inside the mental ward in the hospital. After watching him and observing his actions, they had found out that it was a lie after watching him sitting down in one chair for a great amount of hours with a mean face, looking at the mental patients around him.

However, they still would not release him, unless his mother had come to get him. Therefore, John had called her to come and get him, and she was like hell no. She was not going to go and get him because that was where he needed to be.

Therefore, the only other person that could have come and gotten him out was his mother's ex-husband. John had called him and asked him to come and get him because his mother would not. So he went to take John out the mental hospital and because his mother would not let him back in, John started living with him.

Seizures had continued when he had started going to another school, so John's so-called father was like, "I am going to have to bring you back to your mother's house," because he could not handle those medical bills.

When John had gotten back home with his mother, she was telling him not to unpack his bags because she was going to take him to a homeless shelter.

After a couple of days in the homeless shelter, John did not like it at all because he was sleeping in a room with about eight people, with only one bathroom. John had then started going to another high school named Plantation, which was a bad school, but he preferred that school than South Plantation, the school that his father had put him into. Because in South Plantation he had too many eyes on him, like they had nothing else to do, he was known as a thug with a bad attitude, and in Plantation everyone in there was bad.

John then ran out of the homeless shelter because he did not like there at all. When his eighteenth birthday was right around the corner, his homeboys took him up in his favorite club into which he mostly had to be sneaked in because he was still a minor. However, in that club you had to be twenty-one, but all his homeboys told security was it was their gift to him because they had no money for nothing else. So John was allowed in and given a hundred dollars to do whatever he wanted as they did what they wanted to.

However, John did not spend any of that money; he only watched as others had gotten their fantasies fulfilled. Therefore, one of his friends that was twenty-eight told him, "All right, save your money and I will pay for everything for you." After that night, they were all saying, it was time now for John to start becoming a responsible man. Therefore, they had told John to first move back up north to stay out of trouble and he did, and with one of his homeboys' friend's help, he was able to get back in his mother's house for some time.

John had then went and found a job at Home Depot. When his mother found out, he came home the next day with all of his clothes outside, with all of his mother's locks changed. John began sleeping in one of his friend's car at night and going to work during the daytime while one of his friends was trying to find a room for him to rent out. One was then finally found, so he asked his mother for his bed so that he can have something to sleep on at nighttime. She was so happy that now he won't be coming any more, so she gave him a dresser for his clothes along with it, with his old stepfather's work television.

John started living with a couple that was renting out a room, with its own bathroom. John was satisfied with that room but it was something, he told himself, he was not used to sleeping in a room with no one in there with him to keep him company.

John had then asked his girl Monique, from South Plantation to start sleeping with him because he needed someone to lie down next to at night, to hold and cuddle up with. At first, they were so distant and hardly talking, because she was so far from John.

However, after she started going and spending time with him, she started liking him more, and it all ended up strong and then even greater because her grandmother was a pastor, and her grandmother found out about them too and what John was going through.

Therefore, Monique's grandmother began preaching to John and praying for him every time she saw him. She then began wanting to be there for John, as if he was her own child.

John could never spend a day with Monique while her grandmother was around because she'd just take him away and just talk to him about so many things.

John began telling Monique's grandmother that when he was younger, he was going to church every Saturday and Sunday, believing in and praying to God, every day, but as he got to Him and got to know more about Him, the worse his life was getting, he felt.

"That's what your adversary wanted," Monique's grandmother told John, "so you should have kept going to church, and when your adversary sees that he has no chances of changing you, then he would give up, and then try again in the future, so you should not have not given up."

Monique's grandmother continued preaching to him, telling him never to give up in life because the harder something is in life, the better the outcome is in the end. Therefore, she had told him to never give up no matter what.

Surprisingly, Monique's grandmother never told Monique that John was wishing a future with his best friend. Monique's grandmother asked John out of nowhere one day to truthfully to tell her, whom he truly loved in his life right now.

Monique began getting jealous because now John was smiling in her grandmother's face more than hers. Therefore, she wanted to start having some private time with him. Therefore, she started to skip school and sleeping with John at his place more at nighttime.

They had ended up breaking up after one night she had bit John and he had then bit her back, so she started hitting him constantly because she was a street girl and not expecting John to fight back, so he had hit her back one time on her arms. However, because she was red you could have seen it well. Therefore, he said they need a break and anyway he needs to start working hard again because he was low on his rent money.

Chapter 9

He dreamed and wondered if it would ever come true, asking his Father God for that one, and if he would bring that one person in his life, even if he would have to change his ways. "Have patience and faith, and all you want in life will come to you in time, but not all," he remembered Monique's grandmother tell him. John ended up dreaming about having a girl that he could love, night and day, but he never told anyone because it was not that same girl that he had been talking to now for some time.

Never telling anyone about his dreams and true wants in life, John cried nights, for it all to come someday in his lifetime. He wanted no more friends in his life, other than the ones he had already. They were mostly older than he was, but he had begun seeing them less because of all the distances that he kept traveling.

John had then ended up in a hospital for about a good four months because of so much he wanted and was dreaming of but was stressing him, he was not getting any of the love and treatment that he was wanting from his mother.

John's girl Monique was there sleeping with him every night when she had found out that she was about to have a little John of her own, and his dream.

However, John and Monique had then ended breaking up because he had gotten Monique pregnant. Why? Because he wanted some more people in his life to love, but she had gotten an abortion without him knowing about it all or even making a decision with him.

John did not believe in abortions, and he had told her that and she knew he wanted a child to love. He wanted someone to love in his life, until his time ended because he did not know when his last day was going to be, so he wanted to make sure that he had left a part of him here on earth. However, she had the abortion, and John had meant to get her pregnant at that time, but he had just never told Monique.

Monique was telling John all the time that she had loved him, but she had thought she would have to take care of their baby all by herself and having the memory of John in her mind, she told him.

John had then gotten mad, saying he does not see why girls decide to have abortions, he looks at it like taking another's life for one's worldly happiness. Then saying also that it was either one does not want him/her with that father, or they are not able to take care of their baby because of shortage of money. "You could have given the baby to the homeless shelter, Monique, until we had got on track."

She wanted to be there for John so much, but he was saying that he was sorry for all the distractions that he had given her in her life and that if it was because of money she wanted to make in her life. "Well, go make it then," John told her, they then were there in silence for some time.

John's best friend Tamika and her mother then came to see him. Before Monique had left, they were just looking at each other, wondering about each other.

They already called to see if John needed anything while he was in the hospital, so John was like "Yeah, boxers." When they were there, they had given John some boxers for comfort, instead of being in that long gown with nothing on underneath. John was very thankful and was there talking to Tamika's mother while Tamika went and talked to Monique.

Before leaving, Tamika had given John her first kiss good-bye, John did not grow up being kissed by just a greeting, so he never really greeted another with one.

However, it was "something he had been dreaming of." They were like brother and sister, but only he felt their friendship was a little more.

John then told himself that finally a dream had come true, and that he will never forget that moment because no one will forget a dream come true.

That night, John had fallen asleep with Monique still there just looking at him, but when he had woken up in the morning she was gone.

Monique had left and was never planning on coming back, he had heard from her mother. John had started talking on the phone at night in the hospital bed, with friends but then one mainly, and that was his best friend.

"I will at least try to accomplish this one goal, and that is for this one girl to be the love of my life," John then told himself after a late-night talk on the phone with his best friend.

Every night when they used to talk on the phone, she used to always tell him that she loved him, but he never was truly sure if she truly did because they both were young and she was younger than he was. In addition, thinking that it was only him, she used to smile in front of everyone when he really thought about it, not just him. Therefore, he began to think that she was just telling him that it was only him because she was just trying to make him smile.

Tamika was shy when it came to certain things, but just to make John happy, she would start singing on the phone for him, mainly, all of John's favorite love songs, just to be making him feel special. She then even made that one promise that he had been waiting to hear, and that was "his chance with the one he loved and had began giving his heart to since there was no other."

Nights here lying down unaccompanied, with thoughts of you
Thinking of all the ways you make me feel it deep inside
Feeling there's nothing else to carry out,
Excluding giving my heart and all to you
Eager to be taken as I am
Feeling there's none giving me affection, unlike you
That's why I call for you
Nothing here I require and feel, but you
Feeling so in love with you,
Having me acquainted with,
I will die for your contentment and delight
In your time.

John was then told that he could be released whenever he wanted to because of how calm he was now, with a smile on his face for the first time, since all the nurses known him.

John had then been told that he needed to have surgery, before he left he had to get Ms. Marise's number because she was a caseworker there that had truly cared and had showed love toward John, as if he was her son. John had thanked her for all of she had been helping him out with in there, and she was the one that was there planning his surgery for him, with a doctor that would have done it free for him.

John was like that; he was going to make sure that one day in the future, he was going to get her something for Mother's Day because that's what she was to him in there.

John had then moved in with his homeboy Rob because he had his own place. Starting healthy and fresh again, John was happy and began having faith in his future. However, drama started again on the streets for him, and with his health just back he did not want to be in any.

John stayed in the apartment all the time, but still he then gotten back in the same situations again because fools were coming to their apartment. However, at least he had, had a good week or two of relaxation when he had got out of the hospital because his boy Rob was just there looking out for him.

However, even while he was going through all of those fights and arguments with the people that were living around, it was still all about his best friend, he was saying in his head.

John regretted allowing two of his homeboys to talk to her about his feelings, that it appeared out of nowhere, and he started looking at her differently, more than a friend, and began telling her that he was in love with her.

John began defending her, whenever she would come up in a conversation because he was now in love with her, and he was feeling like he had no other to live for in his life, other than his brothers.

John had planned on never letting her go because instead of crying in corners and in darkness now, John felt he could cry in her arms.

John ended up back on the streets again for some time because he wanted to be near Tamika. Therefore, he started sleeping inside his homeboy Stephan's car again at night. Stephan would just leave it open, and in the mornings, John had to make sure he kept his head down again, so that Stephan's mother would not see him. Whenever she would leave for work in the mornings, and then John would just go and take a shower before Stephan left.

John even went into a gas station one night, asking to use the bathroom outside, and all he did was just open up the bathroom door and then give the cashier back the key, and it was all because John was planning on sleeping in there for the night.

Looking at himself in the mirror that night, he said he deserved to die because of disrespecting his mother so much when he was younger. That he was such a stupid fool, and he had wished that he would just die right then and there, if he were not meant to live a long life.

John then wanted death to just come upon him, balling up his fist, John started to hit himself, and then he just looked at himself in the mirror, and ended up saying, "I hate you, your thoughts and ways." Then he just punched his face in the mirror, breaking the glass. Walking out with his fist dripping blood, everybody that was pumping gas was looking at him.

Living back on the streets, but with his best friend still right there for him and always looking out for him. John never did some of the things he wanted to do and was about to do, not himself but to others because he wanted a future with that one-and-only someday.

Sleeping now in different friends' houses, he wondered if another person had ever had a life like his. John then started feeling worse when he would see a mother kiss her child, then say, "I love you." All he could ever do was close his eyes, telling his Father God good night, and just wish for a future life with that one.

John then moved back in at Rob's apartment because trouble, hate, and anger were everywhere he was going.

John's first argument with Tamika came because she was putting one of John's friend's words, her boyfriend at that time, over his truthful words.

John had caught this boy cheating on her when he and Rob had walked in the house unexpected one night. Everybody was just looking at John laughing, saying, "Here it goes," asking him whom he will choose in this situation because they already knew John did not want him to cheat on Tamika. John had then seen the room door open and three faces coming out with one looking down. They told John that what he was thinking did not happened while they were in the room. However, because the girl did not want John going crazy and asking her questions, she had just told John that "yes, we were having sex in your room."

John had decided to tell Tamika even though that was something that he liked to keep his mouth shut up about whenever it came down to others going through it. However, John loved her, he felt she was worth him and his homeboy's friendship to break apart.

Tamika never believed him though because she put her boyfriend's words over his. John began to wonder what kind of friend does she takes him for truly in her life.

"I gave up a friendship for you and all you have to say to me is shut up, and for me to stop lying to you because his words, the one that you just started talking to, are stronger than mine?"

"Are not we best friends, Tamika?" John then asked her.

"Yes," Tamika said, "but I love him more because he makes me feel better than you make me feel, John, and do not tell me anything like this again because I want to find out by myself."

"Just because he says sweet words to you, Tamika think about it, and ask yourself, what every man wants from a woman."

"He is not like that," Tamika then told John, "I know him, you do not know him like how I know him."

"All right then, Tamika. I will keep my mouth shut then whenever another situation like this occurs," John then told Tamika.

That night, everybody was just laughing and asking John what kind of true friendship does he have with Tamika, his so-called best friend because she did not believe one word that John had told her when he was telling her the truth.

"F—that friendship, John, and go and find a real best friend, that will put trust in your words because I thought that you and her were truly best friends but after that, I now have second thoughts about you and her. How can she put another man's words, she just got into a relationship for about two months or less and they hardly see one another, over a best friend's words whom she almost knows now for over four years."

All John then had to say after that to about ten friends including Tamika's boyfriend was that there is no friendship or relationship perfect in the world and that we all will make mistakes in our lifetime and that he forgives her for that.

John ended up being locked up because he and some of his homeboys had ended up being pulled over one night when they were coming from a football game. The police had pulled them over to question them about their tag because they could not find it in their system. But then again also for the dark tints because the tints that were on the car were limo tints, and they give tickets for tints like that in Florida.

John's boy was like "make sure before we pull over, everybody got every kind of identification out of the car" because it was a stolen vehicle. Therefore, John was saying, "I have not seen all of you in years, and this is how you will reunite with me."

"You're all fools. Go and I will stay because they won't even be able to get no information from me, I do not even know your last names or where you live."

Everybody then ran out and John began saying that he needs a break in life again because when he was in jail the last time, even though it was just for five days, it felt relaxing and helped calm his mind. The police then went after John when he had stepped out of the car with their guns in his face. They started asking John who was the driver of the car, John began saying that he did not know and that they will have to give him that information when they find out.

The police started slamming John on their cars and on the pavement, telling him to tell them or else they'll break a bone in his body. John was just like go ahead, it was going to be paid for by their insurance so he does not care.

Slamming John back and forth on the floor, on the cars and then hitting him in his back and shoulder, John asked the officer if he wanted to fight him because it does not seem like he wanted to arrest him.

"Are you threatening me?" the officer then asked John.

"No!" John then said. "It just seems like you are mad at me right now because I guess your paycheck is going to be less since you did not catch the thief. So now, you are taking it out all on me because I am saying that I cannot tell you their names."

They then arrested John because they had said that he was driving in a stolen vehicle, and if they find any fingerprints on the wheel, John was going to get the time.

However, John already knew the police saw him walking on the sidewalk, and a car had pulled over and had picked him up after the game.

They had then locked up John but they were seeing that he was not really caring how long they wanted to keep him there. He then told the judge at the hearing that he had nothing to say except that he wanted a good bed to sleep on.

Locked up, John only had three people on his mind and thinking what he could do to have a better life when he gets outs. The courthouse had then decided to hold on to him, to see if they held him in jail, he would then decide to talk. Therefore, they transferred John to a jailhouse all the way up north from where he had been arrested from, and it was far from where he was living and walking the streets at nighttime.

John had first started asking himself about how he was going to change, but first he must make a big apology to his Father God. For that day that he was cursing at him and had told him that he was starting to become an unbeliever in Christ.

"I really was not," John had told his Father as he looked up at the ceiling. I was just mad because it just felt like you were just sitting down watching me as I went through all my struggles in life, not wanting to help me."

"I am sorry my father for trying to taking it all out on you because I expected you to help me with each and every trial. However, now I have gotten to understand much more about ones trials in life. It is all just tests, my adversary was just trying to make me fail in my life so that I may not wish to be called your child and a believer in Christ whom truly I know is my Lord and Savior, I know he was and still is the one that has kept me through my years of trials and tribulations."

"I am sorry, Father, for all what I have done wrong and have said, and I repent, Father, and I will do my best to change my life and mind in my time. Lastly, Father, I thank you for bringing Monique's grandmother in my life, with her words to me about being an understanding and knowledgeable young man for making it in life."

Also, giving apology to Tamika as he closed his eyes picturing her in his mind, holding her two hands while face to face saying, "I love you and I wish that I would have been a better best friend in your life. However, no matter what the future holds for you and me, I will always thank and love you for brightening back up my life."

Writing poems about how he felt in his life, and about how he felt about his best friend, about how she had helped him clear his mind. About his past and how Latoya had made him feel better with her time and words of encouragement that he could make it through everything in his life. Latoya was not the only one that had talked to John about his life and ways, there were a lot more but because of his feelings for her, he had more memories and gave more attention to her.

Security guards would ask John what a bad young man like himself know about love and writing about love and that one that he truly feels loves him.

"Are you not supposed to be a thug in here like how everybody else in here is saying?"

"That is how your mind is, right, Mr. Lover Boy?"

One security woman came to read some of what John was writing while the other was talking to him and asking him why he always looked like he wanted to kill someone.

"Listen to this, everyone who thinks John is about to attack them and is wondering about him. It really sounds like he's in love," she then read one letter to everyone in the cell room.

I've always wanted to cry holding you
Not caring what another would say
For every way you've made me feel
When I'd look into your eyes,
But I'd dropped my head,
Fighting every tear, and word,
I wanted to give you
Not another heartbreak
Only someone to love,
I told myself.

I love every smile, and look you give me
Every word and touch, you make me feel
Shivering with joy
An all in one, I think of you
But will you ever be my one?
I'll ask you one day

I love you, I would practice
Night and day
I love you, I would say
But only in my mind,
Whenever she looked at me.

Crying because of all the gladness
She'd make me experience
When I'd walk the streets, thinking
Of every day, every word, every emotion
She had made me feel.

If only I could've had you more
With me telling you that,
I love you.

But now, all I could do
Is cry myself to sleep at night, wishing I could,
Hear the sound of your heart beating,
Telling my Father truly that
I love you.

Security had then asked John if he missed his best friend. John had then just looked up at her and showed her more papers. The security guards had then given John a free phone call, to call someone to come and get him out, so that he can go home and be with his best friend again.

However, John had no one, so he called Tamika, and asked her how was she doing?

Listening to her talk, John had then begun smiling, so the security guard asked him if they needed directions.

John had said no because he was talking to Tamika.

One security guard then looked at him with a tear coming down her eye, saying, "I am going to help you out. However, you have to promise me to do better in life."

"Not try!" With her fingers pointed at John, "Forget what the crowd says about you because they will not be able to be there for you in the end."

The next day, someone came in and questioned John about the case, to see if John had different answers this time, but his answers were all the same. Therefore, they told John that they knew that he knew who was driving and the only reason they wont charge him was because they had been given some of his living situations and it sounded like he had a surgery coming up in two weeks. Therefore, they decided to let him go.

They had then let John out in the middle of the night. Even though he told them that they could have held on to him longer because he felt comfortable in there and that he had two more weeks until his surgery. However, the lady had told him that he had just spent Thanksgiving, Christmas, and New Year's day in jail, so he should go and have some fun before his brain surgery.

Before John left, while they were getting all his things together, they had asked for one more letter, but John was like here take it, but they were like no because John needed to give it her.

Therefore, John read one more to them, and this was the one, he said, that he cried writing:

> Your my dream come true, and I know it takes time, so I'm going to patiently wait, giving up some, giving you a reason to trust and love me, because you've stop my endless tears, misery, pain, feelings of, feeling incomplete with it all at the end, and wanting of that one to love, to hold and never let go.
> I have cherished and have tried to respect every moment we have spent together. I've been scared to make the wrong move at the wrong time, so I'll be here waiting for you, crying days and nights,

waiting for a chance to love you more, and a chance to be your all
because right now you're my everything.
Until then I'll be here waiting alone, not letting anyone else in
because I feel you're permanently my life, and you'll never know how
much tears I've dropped thinking and thanking my Father, just for
you because I'm in with love you.

John then walked for about seven hours straight, not knowing where he was going until the sun came up. John started asking the bus drivers to let him on free because he had just gotten out of jail. So then, he was given a free bus pass to get back home.

John had forgotten all about his surgery because during the time he was locked up, he was not having any more seizures, John was locked up all by himself mostly with just three people on his mind, whom were truly loved by him.

Truly having a wonderful person like Tamika in his life was not ever going to be forgotten about, he said.

That was why he then wished for one wish, and that wish was to become a 100 percent lover, not a fighter. Therefore, he had to figure out how he was going to change himself while not caring what another person might think about him.

When John came out and had gotten back to Rob's house everybody was surprised because they had thought that he was going to be given time.

Tamika was about to have a birthday party before his brain surgery, was all they kept telling him because John was saying that he could not see them after his surgery.

Before John Day came, John had a friend who came on to him, she was about five years older than he was. Thinking that she wanted to have his first child, John went ahead and did it because that was what he wanted and that was to leave a part of him here on earth.

When John went to Tamika's party, none of his friends went with him because he was saying it might be his last time with her, so they stayed home. At the party, John had just sat down wanting to give her all of the letters that he had written but he did not. John just sat down as her friends passed by him, said hello to them because she was beside him. John did not know what to say to her because he was scared that it would be his last night seeing her, so he was just there, fighting each teardrop that was about to fall until he said good-bye.

The next day at nighttime, Violet (their mother and inspiration giver), John, and Rob went in to church for inspiration to them all, but mainly for John though because he was going into surgery the next day.

They all needed prayer because of everything that they were going through in their lives, and were all hoping that John would have made it out of the hospital, the same way he was going to go in.

That night, John read his prayer once more to his Father before he went to sleep, saying mainly that if he made it out, he would love a change in the kind of life he lived and was willing to change himself in process.

CHAPTER 10

The next morning, John went in for brain surgery on January 2006, not knowing if he was going to make it out or not.

In pain for two weeks straight, even on his birthday that had came up a couple days later on February 1, John was in pain wanting just to sleep or die, the left side of his head was swollen, with stitches on it to hold it together.

The hospital wanted to help John because he was there in pain, so they were going to find a nice place for him to stay during and after the pain went away, they knew that he was homeless.

They had said that they were going to help him get on track, and back in school toward a career of his choice. They were also saying that where they were sending John, he was going to be paid each day that he was there. They were going to put a private account for him, so that when he gets out he would be able to have money in his pockets.

Feeling happy about what he was hearing, John had asked a hospital employee where it would be. "Up north somewhere, and if you want, in another state," she said.

Tamika was all he reminded himself about, not even his brothers, because he never wanted to lose her and was willing to make his sacrifices. Therefore, John did not even think about going where they wanted to send him.

John would just be lying down in a bed all day, waiting on doctors and nurses to come and talk, and take care of him, so that was just not for him, John told the lady that was helping him handle his recovery and destination. "Are you sure?" she had then asked, John. "Yes," he told her.

Therefore, John just waited for all the papers that he had to sign and look over, also his release papers.

When he was being released, he did not even call anyone to come and get him, so the nurse was like "are you ready," and he was like, "yeah." First, she was like "let me take something out of you first." John said, "They already took out all of the IVs and needles out of me, so what?"

She was like, "There is one more thing in John that has to be, taken out." Therefore, she lifted up the sheets as if he pregnant and grabbed little John. So John was like, "Shouldn't you lock the doors first," and she just started laughing because all she was doing was taking out something that they had put in little John. So that John would not have to get up and go to the bathroom.

John began going crazy because he had picked up the sheets to see what she was doing. He could not believe they had a little tube in him, and he did not even know it. So he was like, "You will never ever going to put something like that in me again," and to put that in his medical files.

John had then got on the bus to get back to Rob's house. On the bus, they did not even ask him to slide his bus pass or pay them because before the surgery he had an afro that he did not cut, and the doctors had only cut off the side, that they were doing the surgery on. Therefore, John had a half afro with stitches on one side of his head.

Riding on the buses with every person, staring at him, John had felt like a celebrity before he had got to Rob's apartment.

Rob also was just looking at him as if he was a creature that he had never seen before.

John's head was still swollen for about two months straight. John had started giving his Father God thanks more and more each and every day because he had made it through what he had thought he was not going to make it through, and that was part of the reason why he had signed the papers so fast because he was so happy inside, in a way.

After John had gotten a little better, he started looking for a job, and he had found one working at an Ihop, washing dishes, with everyone there also looking at his head, asking him what had happened to his head, and all he would do was just laugh, and say he had a brain surgery five weeks ago.

That's when their eyes would just open up wider and be like, "Shouldn't you be in the hospital?" "Yeah, but I rather work now, and make money," John then told them. "Than stay lying down with things on my mind bothering me because that was part of the reason I had got in that position in the first place."

John had ended up looking for another job because they were not working him enough. He had then found one at a Marriott hotel. It was right by IHop, a couple of streets down from where his mother lives.

The Marriott hotel gave John a job washing dishes because of his bad background because of the problems that he had gotten himself in.

John wanted to be there at the hotel, more than at IHop because it was busier at that time and more hours of work, so that meant more money.

John was busy at the hotel, and also they were offering him much more opportunities of moving up and getting a better position there, so he had to quit IHop to give the hotel all his time.

He had then saved up a good amount of $3,000 in two months because he had no bills to pay, just his cell phone bill, he had now gotten his first mobile phone and it was under his name.

When John had showed it to Alex and Junior, John's two brothers, they had given him a round of applause because he finally got a phone and a job. So they now were like, "When are we going to be getting ours?" they had then said. John then said, "When you start being able to stay out of trouble now, like me." John's brothers were still in elementary school, Alex in third grade and George in fourth grade.

John's brothers not only began calling him to see where he was, but also calling him, asking him for money for anything they saw that they really wanted. John then began buying games for them, whenever they wanted one, or whenever their mother said no.

John then used some of his money to put a down payment on a car for himself because he was in such a rush for his first car. John was so in a rush, that on the first night, as soon as he had gotten his Cirrus, he had gotten a ticket for the lights, the first night he had driven the car.

John did not even make it out of the neighborhood because as soon as he had crossed the main road, lights began blinking behind him. The police had said that he had forgotten to put his left blinker light on, and he had, but then he found that it was not working. So that ended up messing up his night of celebration, well, really his and Rob's night of celebration, they were about to go party.

John had then just turned right back around and right back in their parking lot, and then he went straight to sleep. The next day, after he had woken up in the morning, he went to work at the hotel. He went straight back to the dealer, and was like, "I thought you said that there was nothing wrong with the car?" so the dealer was like "There was not, nothing wrong with it."

"Then what is wrong with the head and backlights," John had then said to him, the dealer had then checked it out, and saw that it was not working right. John had then showed him the ticket, so the dealer was like, "That is not a good sign for you, and your first car." John had then told him, "No! That is not a good sign for your company." John had then told him that he was going to leave the car and that he had better fix it by tomorrow evening.

John had then went to him the next day to get back his car. It was fixed right when John had checked it, so John had then told the dealer, thank you.

When John was about to leave, he had gotten a call back to work to cover for someone that does a different position, which was a house man position, that person could not make it.

John had then started doing houseman duty at the hotel because that person had quit but nobody was really told that.

Therefore, John began unclogging toilets. It was disgusting, but he needed the money. When John had left that same night and was on his way back home, his car started acting up again. However, this time, it was the way that it was driving. Therefore, John asked someone what could be the problem, when he had stopped to see what was wrong with it, and the person was like, "It has to be the transmission."

John had then gotten mad, but he was like, "I am not going to cherish material things." Then this car just came out the gas station so fast, and did not even know that there was a cop right there checking speeds on other cars, so that he could give speeding cars tickets.

The woman had stopped to make a u-turn on a road that was not supposed to be stopped on, so John ended up hitting her car in the back.

John had then gotten even madder because it was only his third day with his first car, and he had already gotten into a car accident.

John did not get a ticket because the woman was making a u-turn in a no u-turn lane. However, through it all both of their cars were undamaged, so John just left after he did all the paperwork.

That incident and the car problems had John just saying forget this car, John then got mad and punched the steering wheel expecting to hear the horn honk, but not even that was working.

The next day, John was so mad that he did not even go to work, John went straight to the man who he thought was the real car dealership manager. John started telling him to give him back all his money, so the dealer started saying that he cannot do that because he was not the real manager there, his wife was, and he would have to ask her first.

The dealer then went up to his speaking in Chinese or Japanese whichever one it was.

"No, sir I cannot do that for you," the man then went back and told John. So John, then asked him why? "Because my wife said no," he said. John then asked him if he was a man or not, the dealer was like, "Yes, I am, but my wife said no, and I do not want to make her mad.'

John then walked away and started just driving around with the car, and letting people borrow it, and after a while he dropped it off and then said thank you for letting me hold your car.

John then started working night and day at the hotel because he needed to make some more money again.

However, John and Rob ended up being kicked out of where they were staying and started living with Rob's cousins.

One day surprisingly, John had gotten a phone call from the man that was being bossed around by not only his manager but also his wife because she was paying all the bills.

He then apologized to his wife, and began saying that he was sorry and that they had fixed the car and for him to come and get the car.

John had then went and they were like, 'Where is the money that you owe us?" John was like, "First I got to make sure it works right this time." Therefore, John told them to give him thirty days, and then he will think about it.

John then ended up being kicked out of Rob's cousin's crib because she had liked him but he just used to ignore her. She had then called one of her homeboys to stay for a while just in case John came back, he would beat John up and then have him scared to be anywhere around her place.

CHAPTER 11

John's job then became his home because John used to sleep in the hotel's used rooms whenever the guest left it dirty. However, he still felt so good in those rooms, especially the beds. John had his own showers at nighttime, and for the first time in years, other than the hospital bed, he slept on a queen-sized bed, and he was by himself which he did not like, but that was all just for one night, then another room with another bed.

Most of the time, the hotel room were sold out because it was mostly a business hotel, and whenever one would do business, they would come all travel together.

That's when he will either sleep in their employee break room or in his car, where all his clothes were at, so that he will be comfortable every night and not lose it, every other night.

After a while, the hotel became too busy for him to be able to sleep in any of the rooms, and for him to be able to take a shower, but he did not care though because even if the guest were still staying there in their rooms, he would have still went in to them to take showers. However, he then changed his mind because he did not want anybody to catching him, and then make a complaint saying that he was going through their belongings in the rooms that they paid for.

Therefore, he started calling his brothers every day, so that they could tell him whenever their mother left the house, and then he would just go and shower at his mother's house. John did not need food because he had enough food at the hotel to eat, all who worked in the kitchen got free food. Especially the kitchen cook, he used to make two orders in one, one for the hotel breakfast and dinner, and one for him and his wife.

Whenever the hotel would get slow again, after an event ended or a holiday, except for on weekends, when it was always busy. John kept spending nights and days there as if he had no life, which he did not, but he still felt like he had nothing else to do except spend time learning more about how to clean. John stayed at work 24/7, telling himself that he was not going to live the kind of life that he was living before he had the surgery, and no matter what he was not going back to the jailhouse even though he loved it.

John would be at the hotel at nighttime in his big bed, by himself, thanking his Father God because he was no longer finding his way into trouble, and not living too much of a stressful life.

He was now there lying down, remembering when he was living with his friends time after time, in different places because each one kept getting kicked out of different places and getting into trouble. There, he was happy now, it felt like the end of all such cases in his life.

John will always have unforgettable times with all of his friends that are now somewhere. Most of them, he does not even know where they could be because of the things most of them have done in their lives and had said that they were going to continue doing it all.

A couple of days later, John's brothers had called him, telling him that we have a cousin now here from Jamaica, who was now moving in with their mother, and had been asking about him because she wanted to meet and talk with him about helping her out with a job at the hotel he was working at.

Her name was Joyce, and she was a very kind and loving family member he had heard. Joyce and John then met up a couple of days later because he had been busy at work. Joyce and John had then gotten to know one another well.

Therefore, Joyce started trying to help him out as much as she could because she found out he was living at the same place he worked at and why he was not living with his mother, from one of his mother's friend that his mother had introduced to her.

Joyce had then finally found out all the information, and what was going on between him and his mother, from him, so she was like, "Try one more time to have a relationship with your mother," and he did, too easily. Finds out, it was just because his mother was having money problems at that time and she did not want to lose her home.

Therefore, John's mother really wanted money from him, and for him to pay the water bills and electricity bills because she was living in an area that hard workers live at, not people that only work when they want new accessories on them or in their home.

She was low on her monthly bills because she was spending too much of that child support money that she was getting on foolishness.

John's mother allowed him to rent out one of her rooms in her new house. In addition, he had to buy food and drinks for the house weekly, and that was the main complaint he was making because he was hardly there during days and nights. He still was working hard and all day at the hotel. Even while John had a room to sleep in, John still slept at the hotel because he was so used to it already.

John had then heard that it was because she had no GED that she was unable to work in the medical fields that she was trying to get into. Therefore, John then helped her get an online diploma that she had seen come in the mail for him because he was being given a position that required a diploma.

Therefore, she had asked him to take the test for her too, so he had then taken it online for her.

Surprisingly, John had passed the test for the second time, but for her his mother this time. However, he was still feeling proud of himself. So now, with the diploma, she was able to get a better job in the nursing field. John's mother had then gone back for the job that they had told her that she was not qualified for, now that she had what they had asked for, they had then given her a chance in the field that she wanted.

John had then began to wish that he had never did that because his mother then wanted to kick him out the house again, the job she had been wanting was now given to her, so she was now back on track.

However, she wanted John out so fast, John started to pay less because he was putting some money away for a good car, also for a room that he wanted to rent out.

John had then asked her to give him a couple more weeks, but she had said no, but he already knew what he had to do.

John had then went to Joyce and told her what she had said, when she was not around to defend him.

After Joyce had talked to her about letting John stay until he saved up the amount he needed, she just began ignoring John whenever he spoke to her. Every day she was telling him that his days at her place were numbered, and for him to hurry up and get out of her presence.

John had already returned the Chrysler Cirrus because it began acting up again. However, when he had gotten the amount he had needed, he had started financing a new Impala, when he had saved up all the money that he had needed to put a down payment on it.

When John's mother had seen it, she was amazed because she just looked at it and then said, "Ok, you can go now."

John had then told her that he needed to find first a room to rent out. Therefore, she was like hurry up before she gets mad. John had then found a room nearby, about two weeks later online, so he then moved out and started his life on his own again.

When John was packing up and leaving, John's mother had told him that she did not want him back over her house anymore since he was going to his own place now. However, John still went over there because that was where all his mail was going and only when his brothers were there.

John had then stopped going for a while because he had a nighttime job now at a Chilli's restaurant. After work, he started to become very tired. Therefore, John would end up going home, and just writing and talking to himself about things he was now hoping to accomplish in life, and asking himself when would be the best time to ask that one, if she would love to come into his life, now.

John would write and listen to love songs, whenever he did not work or go out.

One day, after listening to a preacher preach about giving God thanks for life no matter what, "Even if we are one step away from death?" John asked himself.

John then started writing to himself saying, "Many people that know me, may not believe me. When I say that I pray every night and day giving God thanks for all he had brought me through, and for where I am today, even though I still go through trials. I thank God for the mindset that I have now grown, seeking achievement, and success in my life today, for a better future for myself and a better chance of getting that one I love. Meant to be or not, I won't step back from that one I love, I once told myself because I know my Father understands and I'm asking my Father for that chance."

While working at the Marriott hotel and at the Chilli's restaurant, and having no free time in his life, John regretted it in a way because he rather to have fun nowadays in life because of what he had been through.

Rethinking about it all, John told himself that it was what he had been through and experienced that had truly helped him to have a mind of understanding about other people and the world.

John had no time to think about or worry about the past or future anymore. But then again, it all had him saying in his mind that this was all too good to be true, and that one mess up could end it all, he felt.

Having it all good and going well for him.

He then told himself that if any more tribulation arrives, he would be ready, ready with his Father at his side.

John kept telling himself that he will be ready for any trial working its way into his life, but he never thought that it would ever come—with his best friend parting, out of his life.

Even though she kept on saying no, he did not say or do this. He knew she was not telling the truth because of not just other people's words to him, but also her words and interest in him in each one of their situations.

John called her one day because he was down the other hallway at the end, and she was at the other end of the school hallway with her friends, but she did not know that he was there.

John saw her just pick up her phone, and looked at the name and just dropped it back down on her bag. Now, when he had called her from his friend's phone, whom she also knew, but was loved by many girls, she picked up.

John had asked her why didn't she pick up his phone call, she responded that she never saw his name come up on her phone, "So I don't know what you're talking about," she responded back to John.

"OK, bye," John then said to her, with his friend laughing at him, beside him, telling him that he had been told by him to get Tamika out his mine and look for another, "But no, you want to do what John wants to do." Why? Because John believed Tamika loves John the same way that John loves Tamika.

John had ended up calling her that same night and asked her if she still wanted to be friends with him, and she responded, "Yes, John!" However, it sounded like Tamika just said it so that she will not break his heart because she knew that is what he wanted to hear.

John had felt as if she wanted to leave his life now, and wanted more time for herself and her other friends.

Coming from work that Friday, Joyce, John's cousin asked him if he could drop her off at his mother's house because her car, the one she had bought, was not working right. "Anyways," she then said, "mail is on the counter top waiting for you."

John then told himself that he was not go there and eat his mother's food, or touch anything that was not his.

When they had got there, John's brothers were on the computer, so he had just went and sat down on the couch, talking to them about why they be loving that MySpace website thing so much, and if they did not have homework to do or a girl to talk to on the phone.

John's cousin was in the kitchen looking for some food to eat, however she could not find anything that she wanted at that time. So Joyce asked John's mother, where all the food at because she could not find anything that she wants to eat.

John's mother had went in there telling her that if she cannot find anything to eat, John probably already went in there, and took it and put it in his car to take home because that is all he do, come in and take her food, and then say that he never did it.

John then just looked at her and asked her, why every time if something is broken or missing, he gets the blame, and then she tell everyone about it, and then go to him about buying it all back, and he was not even there.

"You do not ever tell the truth about anything that you do and know," John's mother then said.

"Why should I be scared to tell you if I touch something so stop saying that, and no, that man was not cheating on you because of me," John then told her.

John's mother then turned to her cousin, and was like "Do you see how he talks to me?" and that she was going to call some man that she had a crush on to come and teach him a lesson about talking back to her and lying to her about things that he did and knew.

"Why do you keep bringing up the past, and I am not lying to you," John told his mother. "My baby is going to come for you," John's mother kept saying to him.

John was then like, "I cannot take being threatened, when people think I fear anything about them, another or death."

Therefore, John just took his mother's phone off the counter and found the name Donald her Boo, and then called him, he had then asked for Donald when he had picked up, and then asked him when was he coming to come and teach him a lesson?

Donald then surprisingly told him that he was going to come, and teach him a lesson about disrespecting his mother.

John then told him that he will be waiting and then cursed him out, and told him to make sure when he comes, he will be able to fight like a gladiator because only one will be making it back home.

John's mother then took the phone from him, and tried calling Donald back, but he was not picking up, so she got mad at him and started telling her cousin that this was exactly why, she does not want Jonathan here, at her house.

John had told her to stop saying things that are lies about him because truthfully he cannot take any more ones like that in his life.

John's mother started saying that she does not care what John says to her because he was the devil, and all he did were evil things like, lying, disrespecting, and irritating her.

"You have messed up my life since you came out of me, and into this world as my child," John's mother then told him. John's mother then stood up, looked into his eyes, told him to go back to hell and out her life.

John started saying to Joyce, "Even though it was wrong of me to curse that man out like that. I did it because last time she had put Donald on the phone with me, he was saying stupid things to me, trying to get me scared, and I wasn't ready for him at that time because I had just came out of jail and had some problems on the street. However, now I want to release it, instead of adding it to my list of problems."

John's argument with his mother kept on going until John could not take it no more. When he was about to get up and just leave her complaining about him, he heard his mother say that he was the reason why her life was like this, again.

John then told Joyce, "I am the reason why my mother's husband left her so fast, huh Joyce, so that is the reason why she wants me out her life."

"I am the reason why he left you, and you are so mad, well then kill me then," John then told his mother.

"I am the reason for all you have went through, and lost. Why cannot you truthfully tell people why you are so mad at me? Huh!"

After those words, John's fist just flew through her big screen television, and he knew she was going to call the police.

Therefore, he left and went to the room that he was renting out, and got some money for her big screen television. Then he dropped his car off at his homeboy Stephan's house, and just left the keys in his mailbox, and called Stephan and told him, where his keys were, and if he had gotten locked up, to come get him out, and then he will pay him back.

When John had gone back to his mother's house, the police was already there. So all he did was just give them his hands, and was like, "Are you going to arrest me?"

They then were like that they have no reason to arrest him, yet. In addition, the woman officer winked at him because she remembered that he was the one that they had found running, when they had caught him sleeping in the park one night, well, not her, but his name and face was in investigation.

The officers then just wanted him to give his mother the money for her big screen television, and then left. They had also said that he had to stay a couple of feet away from her house until the case she was starting, finished.

That night John asked Tamika, if they could go to the movie together and talk for once. However, she told him no because she had things to do. Then when he went over to his homeboy's house, and asked him where his sister was? He told him that they all went to the movies together. With whom, John asked him. My sister, your best friend, her sister, and a couple others, he told him.

John then just told him bye, with tears coming down his eyes, telling himself he wants out of this dramatic life because he cannot even get that one he has been loving for some time, other than his brothers, who were with their mother, and his Father GOD, who was not visible, and unable to hold.

CHAPTER 12

The next day, when John had gone to work at Chilli's, mad and not wanting to speak to anyone just to work, John had still held in everything inside, from the day before and that was not good.

The restaurant had started to become busy after 7:00 p.m., so more dishes were coming to John and that meant he had to start moving faster. However, while he was working hard and fast, a male server had just thrown a dirty plate in the sink, and water had splashed on John. John had then looked at the waiter with aggression wanting to go after him, at first, his co-worker told John to ignore it but John could not.

John had thrown down his gloves and went after him, and pushed him and had told him to apologize, but the waiter never wanted to, so John said all right.

When the manager saw John already mad, he was already coming out of the office, to see what was wrong. Right before John had raised up his arm to hit him, John's manager had pulled him back, and asked him to come in his office with him, to talk to him, asking him, "I thought you were not going to be acting this way if I hired you?"

"Is not that what you had told me when I had asked you if you had a short temper?" John just looked at him and then just walked right out the office door, and then out the restaurant's back door because he said he did not want to work and be there anymore.

Then at work the next day, during a weekly meeting for improvement of each associates duty, so that the hotel could be on its way up to a five star hotel. The manager had wanted John to start cleaning the kitchen backroom and prepping area because the chef was not doing his job right.

However, when the chef heard that, he was like no, he knew that meant less hours of work for him.

The chef had then said that it was because he was the one cooking in the kitchen, so of course he was going to need to know and make sure that he knows where each item was, whenever he was preparing a meal for a guest.

John then said, 'Yeah, all right, I understand, go ahead and continue cooking and cleaning in your own kitchen." He had already made himself up doing all the banquets and meetings for both of the Marriott hotels.

However, the manager did not want that because he was not, liking how the hotels kitchen was looking. So he told John it was not the chef's decision it was the manager's decision.

But then the chef started saying that he does not want John working back in the kitchen because he will be stealing all of his food and scaring away all of his customers.

When John had heard that, John had just started to flip, if John would have known how to control himself, whenever he gets mad at another because he does not like to be blamed for untrue things. So that all reminded him about his mothers words about him, to others that were all lies.

John could have gotten that chef fired for a fact because of all the money he had used, buying grocery for his house, and materials the chef had stolen from out of the hotel's storage for his house.

However, John then just snapped and got mad, and then walked out. At first, he was just going to go in his car and drive away, but he decided to go back in the meeting for payback. However, the maintenance manager was just there asking him what was wrong, and for him to come back to work the next day, since he was so mad.

John had then just decided that he could not take being stressed no more, so he told them bye.

John ended up losing both his jobs in one week after the fight with his mother. He went to each job starting fights because he did not want to be taken as nothing, and could not take people lying in his ear or around him.

John's mother had then wanted to put a restraining order on him since she was finally given the opportunity, the police told her that it was the only thing she could do to him.

Therefore, John had gone into court and had told the judge to go ahead and give it to him because he does not care. Now, he could not go back to her house or else he was going to be arrested each and every time he stepped a certain distance from her house.

It became really hard for him to be able to find another job because of his record. So the best thing that he could do to get one was to go to an agency for help.

John had still kept it in mind that he wanted to seek a brighter and happier future in his life. Therefore, he began looking for a bigger job to do.

A job with a career attached to it, to help him achieve a better future and opportunities greater than he expects to achieve while doing that one job.

John began asking himself questions night and day.

"How am I going to find it?"

The first thing that had came to mind was having fun while he was making money and having the right mind in it, while wanting to achieve greater in it.

But while having all these thoughts, one thing he felt and knew was that money does not bring happiness, even though it seems to at the beginning.

Working with an agency during the days that he could, even though he already had money in the bank, but at the same time, he wanted more money to start something going right in his life again, anyways he still needed more money to keep paying his bills.

At nighttime, he started to do that one thing to help him have an idea of a better character for himself, and that was reading love books, so that he could really know what a woman's mind is consists of, but he already knew, not every woman's mind is the same.

John still had his car, so he started going out to different places by himself, and just having a wonderful time with people that he had met that same night, he wanted to start meeting new people.

He started to meet back up with some of his friends from all over, and he could not believe what he heard some say. Some believed that he had passed away because of the health condition that they knew he had, and some were just saying that they had heard that he could not be found anywhere anymore.

John had met up with his little sister Alicia that had gone off to college.

Alicia had from time to time called and checked up on him to see how he was doing. Therefore, John started doing the same, also making sure that no man was doing her wrong. That was why she never really told him about any of them. She was like a little sister to him because they first had a good friendship while he was talking to her best friend Cindy, but their friendship had continued even though his relationship with Cindy ended.

However, Tamika's little sister Carol was much more of a sister for John because she was so much more younger.

Even though she was like five years younger than John was.

Carol began also being an older sister toward John because she was always telling him things that he could not do and words he should not say. He always felt happy around her because he felt she was going to be a real person in life. However, after time it all changed, just like with him and Tamika.

Why didn't I realize and say the things that I needed to say?
Why didn't I apprehend and do the things I needed to do?

Why didn't I show and give her my heart, body, soul, and mind that
I've now developed in me, because of all my,
Trials and tribulations,
In life.
John wrote one night, about that someone he misses so dearly.

Alicia had felt that John was a little lonely in life, and he was seeking happiness in his life with another. Since everyone were saying that he had no chances with that one he was in love with and crying for. Alicia had then said, "I am going to introduce you to my friends from up north, and you decide."

Alicia never wanted John to talk to one of her friends again because he already had talked to one. However, she still ended up introducing him to one of her friends, whom he heard felt attracted to John, when she had seen his picture.

Therefore, Alicia told Natalie, her friend, a little bit about John. Alicia described him as a nice guy with a changed mind in life because of the whole fact of that he kept telling her, that he was trying to live a right life. However, first she made sure he was not talking to any girls, so she went through his phone.

Then the next time Alicia was with her friend Natalie, she asked her if she wanted to be introduced to him now. Her friend Natalie said yes, so Alicia called John and introduced them, and then she said, for now, to do the rest by themselves.

Her name was Natalie, so he was thinking she was a good girl. She was a nice girl who was looking for that right one to also come in her life. She had sounded delighted to hear from him. Nevertheless, he believed that he was more delighted because he was feeling that he needed someone more than she needed anyone.

John and Natalie ended up talking on the phone that same night, all night, telling each other about each other and what has been going on in each other's lives. John then was thinking that they were probably not meant to be with each other because they first started over the phone, and he believed the best ones were face to face.

Two days later on a Thursday night, some men tried to rob Natalie's check-cashing store, so she said that she needed someone to be there for her, and hold her, and to put a smile back on her face, so she wanted to spend a couple of days with him.

The first night she came over, John slept on the floor because he only had a twin-size bed, and he wanted to give Natalie her space. Then the second night, after an all-day, all-night talk with each other, she felt that she could trust him, so she told him that she wanted him to sleep on the bed with her.

However, there was no way to stay inches away from her, therefore she felt all of John's body parts. They then ended up kissing each other, after a good five-minute talk with straight eye-to-eye contact.

Every second, their lips began getting closer together, as they were having conversations with each other, until they just began kissing.

John and Natalie spent the whole weekend together surprisingly in one place talking. They were getting really close with each other, so he told himself that third night with her that he was going to just be himself, to see how deep this one now in his life would end up.

Still pursuing that bright idea that had popped up in his head day by day, with her at his side. He had no distractions from her at that moment, only her influence of doing it all right and well in life.

It all went to an end because he felt that the perfect ones in a moment were sometimes the wrong ones in disguise and because of her I'm-the-boss-so-listen-to-me personality. He did not care about the making out part, every moment and time she wanted to, it was her "do this when I tell you to."

John had stood strong, and did not let it stress him and just moved on day by day just looking at her and ignoring her whenever she had been mad for something small.

Telling him to wait and have faith for achievement in his life, and to no longer give one his heart until they have become one.

Even though it is a better decision at times to take chances in certain matters because he may never know the outcome of it all, and it may become more than he ever expected.

John and Natalie ended up breaking up because John could not take her attitude any more, over time. John had told her that she was too beautiful for him and that she deserved better than him in life. In addition, saying he hopes that she would find that one that will love her for the way that she was and just for pleasure and joy.

Acting as if she did not care if John left her or not, Natalie walked out the door saying the same things again. Telling John, that he will never find another female like her again in his lifetime.

"Yes, that is true, Natalie. As a matter of fact, I have known someone greater." John had told Natalie.

Twenty minutes later, John had gotten a phone call from her saying that she had just gotten into a car accident on the highway.

So John had then called one of his friends to take him to the accident scene but by the time they had reached there, everyone was gone. John had then called and asked her where she was and she gave the name of the hospital.

John's friends had then dropped him off at the hospital and then left him there because he had told them that he would just take the bus home.

Seeing her in there, John was speechless, not knowing what to say except to ask her if she was doing alright now.

Looking at him, Natalie then started putting all of what just happened to her on John because John had allowed her to leave instead of pulling her back in the house asking her to stay. However, he said nothing because he just wanted to know if she was alright and if she had called her family also.

No! She then had told John because she did not want her family to know. So she only had called another friend to come and take her home after the doctors released her.

Having an injured neck the doctors had then told her, after examination Natalie still wanted to go. So the doctors gave her what she needed, which was the neckband around her neck and then told her that she could go. John had called her family home secretly and had told them what happened.

So as soon as she was ready and about to leave the hospital, her family then walked in, wanting to know all of what happened to her.

John had then taken the bus back home before it had gotten too late. Walking in his home finally after a long walk, John had received a phone call from Natalie mad and upset, asking John if he really cared for her. He had not even called her, and asked her if she had made it home safely or not.

"Why should I?" John had then asked her. "And you did not even want me to meet your family."

Natalie had not wanted her family to see him or meet him, so she had told him to go the other way. However, the one thing that she did not know was that John was the one talking to them first about what happened to her after introducing himself over the phone and directing them to the hospital that Natalie was at.

Telling John that she felt loved and cared for in her home so she does not need him anymore in her life. However, when she had gotten better and had stopped being babied by her family, Natalie called John, asking him if he needs her back in his life.

John had then told her no because his bed and pillow right now were all he needed and of course his Father God at his side.

"Oh yeah! Natalie, I finally see why you expect it all your way and how you say it to be. That is because you're the baby out of over five sisters and a couple of brothers included but different mothers. So no, I will not be the soldier in war, and you my captain," John had then told her. "So I must say bye."

Thinking truthfully of a true and right girl, no one else came in his mind again but Tamika.

John never wanted to give up on Tamika because he was just going to give her space and her time with whomever, even if it was for five to ten years. Hoping no one will get her pregnant or make her feel those same feelings that he feels for her.

Learning mostly about love from another, John learned that if that love gets too strong, it'll tear one down—if it doesn't go right like how one was expecting it all to go.

However, our Father's love will always be there no matter what, who, when, and where. Therefore, if he wishes to give one his life and everything else, his Father would be that best one.

Nightly asking what's going to happen in the end as a brother grows living a life of sin and a brother's mind blown from love.

John loved and wanted Tamika still, even though he felt that all his roads were going to end because of all the happiness he wanted to bring in her life as payback. Saying that, out of many, she was that one to replace his grandfather's love.

However feeling now,

Weakening me now
She once made me strong
Not liking each other
She made me love her
Hating the world
She made me love it
Because she was a part of it

All the damages
That I now feel
She has done to me
In the end
I still feel to thank her
Where would I now be in life?
I ask myself
Would I still be here?
For this special one today
That I now have in my life
Whom is now
Myself

Living now with the feeling of having nothing or anyone there by his side, wondering. Who is he now going to be in life? Writing poems, and his first book ever about his life, for inspiration toward goals in life. Toward not only him, but also others having a hard time prospering, achieving in life, losing hope in their lifetime.

Wondering what was next to come and telling himself,

I was not ready to live a life in misery, because of such huge fields of
love that I grew up in with no one trespassing, trying to annihilate
my field.
Having walls built for protection, for a strong and loving future for
myself from not only damage but also a total loss.
Nevertheless, now living having walls that I've felt could never be
rebuilt in my time.
I still believe that!
I will fight back, and make it through all my trials and tribulations
with my Lord Father God by my side.

In addition, for all of whom I have watched, questioned while
sleeping on the streets and for those that are struggling in life for
happiness because of not love, but money, I say for you to the world.
Give more, so that we can build more, put interest in
understanding another more in whatever actions one might
carry out in life. Because we all are fighting for survival against
adversaries and are sometimes falling but if we stand together and
help shield and strengthen one another imagine the world that we
will live in together, having more happiness with one another, at
one another's side.
That is how I
Jonathan Anthony Burkett
Feel
GOD BLESS US ALL

Here I am today, hoping that this book will start something bright, and right in my life. I've spoken to others about my life, and now I've told you how my life has went, and truly how I fell and gotten backup, with the help and the love given to me from my Father God in heaven.

I've shed my tears throughout my life, not telling no one until it was too late. I fell, thinking I wasn't going to be making it back up by myself, but each time, it wasn't me, God had another to come and help me back up, and I have asked for his forgiveness in life, for each time I've doubted him.

I've learned that if you're looking, and constantly wanting for that one to come in your life, to give you all the love you felt that you've lost and you're now deeply seeking for it to come back in your life. It'll tear you down if you let that wrong one in deeply inside you, never expecting for that one to ever let you go.

But our Father's love will always be here for us, no matter what, who, when, and where. I've learned that when I felt that there was no one here for me, and I couldn't even get that one. Even though he is not visible, I've just believed that he has been with me holding my hands day and nighttime.

Continuously making mistakes, feeling sad, vanquished, troubled, sorrow, terrified, interrupted, and frustrated through all devastating circumstances, and tragedies.

Remember no one is perfect, and we all will make mistakes in our lives. Especially, when we have finally taken our Father as our all in life. Therefore, just have faith in our Father God and then after, all is said and done. We will all be celebrating a great victory because we all have overcome all adversaries trying to steer us in another path for happiness. So that we may not enter into our mighty Father God's kingdom.

Why?

I'll never be loved and cared for again
When I had finally realized, that,
That one, was now parted out of my life

Having times of not only believing it
But also hearing it, from another
That no other will ever love me

Thinking it, also hearing it
That I was no longer loved and wanted
Brought not only tears down my eyes at night

But sleepless nights, with no other
There to hold me, and wipe my tears as I trembled
Not only nights, but also in light

Asking why? You had to leave me,
So sad, and lonely with no other here
Who truly loves, and care for me
Like you do?

Truthfully

Not knowing me
But wanting to be there for me
Is a reason why
I'll never forget about you
And will always continue loving you

Granting me your attention
Knowing there were others, more important than me
Have me now with an extraordinary feeling
That will always stand strong in my body, heart, and mind

Having me now feeling
That it was, because of you
I was able to make it through
Wanting to live my life again
Except, rightly

That is why I feel, truthfully
Because of your desire to love and care for me
Is why I feel
My heart is in your hands
And truthfully
"I Love You"

No chance with that one I love

Thinking that she was, that one for me
Has broken my heart
To hear her say
It'll never be

Crying days and nights
I just wanted that one to be
That one love

It was all that I wanted
And if I could've, I would've
Let the whole world know
That I've fell in love
With that one, that has
Brought, light back into my life

Brotherly, sisterly love yes that one love
I've prayed
Nights and days for
Time after, time because
"I Love You"

The one holding you
Loving you passionately
Is the one
I'm hoping to be
Someday

Feeling you
Deep inside my heart
No one
Could ever change my mind
Making me not loving you
Sacrificing all
No matter what may be
That outcome of it all
For the reason that
In my heart
I feel
I'm falling in love
With you

Taking it as a lesson learned
For one reason that
My eyes remained wet
Never dry
For you
Not coming in
My Arms

Learning not only to Forgive
As well forget
Hence that
Countless tears
May well not
Plunge down my eyes
In hours of darkness
As well as brightness
In favor of
You
The one I had chosen
To be devoted to
My entire lifetime

Notwithstanding,
Dreams now and then
Do come true
Which why mine would remain
To love you
The one
I've long for

Lonely just for you
Wanting never, another
To hurt you
Similar to
How I've been
Shattered

Thanking you still
For your times
Standing by me
With care
In our friendship

Your smile
Impacted my heart
Your tone
Sweet with inspirational words
Eyes
Glistened in light
Having me feel
You were my sunshine
Lifting me up with faith
However
Holding me
Never wanting me
Out of sight and in your life

You loved me
And held onto me for so long
I felt blessed
Like no other

Feeling blessed
Thanking my Father
For just that one
Not even
My life

Wishing things would've happened
Another way
Insisting still,
However knowing
It's all thrown out
My door

Wanting such love
For so long
Crying now, deep inside
Asking that one in mirrors
How could you let an angel go?
Why didn't you say the words you needed to say?
Changing
Being that one
She wanted you to be
Expecting her back
Stay, torn apart
Expecting her life
To be
Your life

Destined To Be

A new direction?
Yes, I think it's time
Find a new direction?
Can I?
Must I?
For I don't want to, waste no more time

First admitting my wrongs
And making them right

Then taking the time
To show myself
I'm not lying

Individually, I know I must grow
For when no one's around
I will know what to show

Respectfully, I know I must grow
For I will do unto others
What I wish unto me
For fellowship is what I see best

Jealous of love?
I once was
Till I was reminded
His love will never go

Down the valley
Into the dark
I shall never go

But up the hill
And into the light
I shall be

In a new direction
I must go

Finding prosperity
And not destruction

Finding fellowship
And not hatred

Finding light
And not darkness

Finding right
And not wrong

And finding love
Instead of none

A change in life
I must see
To show myself
Through all
Truly, I was destined to be.